ABRAHAM LINCOLN
THE CHRISTIAN

BY
WILLIAM J. JOHNSON

mm mott media
BOX 236, MILFORD, MI. 48042

BOOKS BY WILLIAM J. JOHNSON

ROBERT E. LEE THE CHRISTIAN
GEORGE WASHINGTON THE CHRISTIAN
ABRAHAM LINCOLN THE CHRISTIAN

TO
MY WIFE
ADVISER, HELPER, CRITIC
THIS BOOK IS
AFFECTIONATELY DEDICATED

CONTENTS

The crowning glory of Abraham Lincoln was the grandeur of his Christian character.
—*Rev. William Bishop, D.D.*

WHY

"LINCOLN, the Lawyer"; "Lincoln, the Citizen"; "Lincoln, the Story-Teller"; "Lincoln, the Statesman"; "Lincoln, the Friend of Man," and other phases of this remarkable character, have received special treatment at the hands of various students and writers. While some attention has been given to the religious side, it has been comparatively meager, and has not received the prominence that it deserves.

Sixteen years ago, as Lincoln's Birthday drew near, I was astonished to hear and read so much that he was an infidel, atheist, deist, Universalist, Unitarian, Spiritualist, etc. Although I was a great admirer of him and had studied his life, having been born and brought up not very far from his Indiana home, up to that time my attention had not been directed to his religious beliefs. It seemed to be taken for granted that he was a Christian, but I was not able to meet the statements of those who declared that he was not.

Here was one of the world's greatest characters: could such a character be the product of unbelief? Here was a definite effect: what cause could produce it? What was the source and strength of the marvelous personality and character of Abraham Lincoln?

These questions led to a careful study of his life, writings, and speeches, to find what Lincoln had said that would reveal, if possible, his own mind and heart. The result of the first brief study was given in an address on Lincoln's Birthday. It was in a community saturated with unbelief in matters of religion. The people seemed amazed, yet pleased, that there was so much evidence of his Christian belief.

During all these years I have been on the alert for anything I could find in public addresses, papers, magazines, and books bearing upon the subject. Almost every year the address has been given in part on Lincoln's Birthday. Always the people have urged that it be put in book form, and so made permanently accessible to the public.

In the beginning, not expecting to publish it, many notes were made without preserving the source. Consequently, there may be quotations found in the book without being so indicated. For this I humbly beg the pardon of the authors, whoever they may be, assuring them that my only purpose has been to let their more apt expression of the thought continue on its mission of good. "The words of Lincoln and the incidents in his life are the property of the world—belong to no person, nor covered by any copyright."

In the hope that others may be interested in studying the religious side of Mr. Lincoln's life, references to the sources of information are given in the back of the book. Everything is believed to be authentic. The greater part is Lincoln's own recorded words. While it must be admitted that in the "reminiscences and recollections" of his friends the memory is not always accurate, yet everything is in harmony with other things which are accepted by all as authentic.

The chronological order has been followed, so as to show his religious development. To aid the reader, the year associated with the matter presented is given at the top of the page. There are some things, however, the date of which cannot be determined, and therefore no year is given. Many of the longer quotations from Lincoln appear in smaller type, without quotation marks.

Here ends a labor of love. The aim has been to let Mr. Lincoln speak for himself, that the people, hearing his message, may learn to know the real Lincoln.

Since the beginning of the Christian era, among them that are born of women there hath not risen a greater than Abraham Lincoln.

W. J. Johnson

Merriam Park,
Saint Paul, Minnesota,
April 25, 1913.

INTRODUCTION

IN writing a book on Abraham Lincoln, the Christian, the Rev. William J. Johnson has set himself a notable task, and done something well worth while. And he has not slighted the subject, but has studied it in its entirety, and produced a book that will delight all friends of Mr. Lincoln, and ought to have a wide circulation. He shows Mr. Lincoln to have been not an atheist, nor an infidel, nor an agnostic even, but a profoundly religious man—a God-fearing, a God-praying, and a God-trusting man—believing implicitly in a Supreme Power in this universe "that makes for righteousness," and relying confidently on His overruling providence and divine guidance. If not our "first American," clearly Mr. Lincoln was one of our first—a great and typical American, not inferior even to George Washington on many lines. Or, as Lowell well said, "he was one of Plutarch's men"—one of the kind of heroes and great men old Plutarch loved to gossip about, and his name will remain "a flag among men," around which men will rally and fight for God and humanity, until the last syllable of recorded time.

> His good sword is rust,
> His bones are dust,
> His soul is with the saints, I trust.

I count it among the greatest of my honors to have walked by his side, and shaken hands with him, and conversed with him face to face; and may God bless his memory forever!

JAMES F. RUSLING.

Trenton, New Jersey,
February 17, 1910.

FOREWORD

It was my privilege as a young man to have known Abraham Lincoln. Entering the service of the United States government in the fall of 1863, the first Sabbath of my sojourn in Washington City I went to the New York Avenue Presbyterian Church. When the time for the long prayer came, according to immemorial usage in many Presbyterian congregations, a number of the men stood up for prayer, and among those upright figures I noticed in particular that of the President of the United States. As a member of the New York Avenue Church I was seated not far from Mr. Lincoln at Sunday services for a year and a half, and his attitude was always that of an earnest and devout worshiper. He was also an attendant at the weekly meeting, though for a considerable period taking part in the services privately. It having become known that he was an attendant at the prayer meeting, many persons would gather in or near the church at the close of the service in order to have access to him for various purposes. Desiring to put an end to these unwelcome interruptions, the Rev. Dr. Phineas D. Gurley, the pastor of Mr. Lincoln, arranged to have the President sit in the pastor's room, the door of which opened upon the lecture room, and there Mr. Lincoln would take a silent part in the service. He informed his pastor on several occasions that he had received great comfort from the meetings, and for the reason that they had been characterized more by prayer than by the making of addresses.

Dr. Gurley bore repeated testimony to myself and to other members of the church of the deeply religious character of Mr. Lincoln, and it is with pleasure that I add this brief testimony from my own experience and observation to the far more extended tributes to Mr. Lincoln as a Christian given in this work, reverently prepared by my colaborer in the kingdom of God, the Rev. William J. Johnson, D.D.

It will be fifty years next fall since I came into direct touch with the man, who in the providence of God was the liberator of a race, and I shall always hold in sweet and blessed memory my first sight of him, as a devout worshiper standing for prayer in the sanctuary of the Most High.

WM. HENRY ROBERTS,

Stated Clerk of the General Assembly of the Presbyterian Church in the U. S. A., Philadelphia, Pennsylvania, November 26, 1912.

A TESTIMONY BY MR. LINCOLN'S PRIVATE SECRETARY

No man can lead two lives or spiritually serve two masters, although, by special effort or otherwise, he may seem to do so. Abraham Lincoln lived but one life. It was even singularly open, unconcealed, easily to be read and understood. The character-istics of that life, all its wonderful story, from birth to death, have been recorded, searched, printed, to the last degree of even scientific analysis. Its every freckle or wrinkle has been noted, whether for good or evil. Therefore it is now too late for any new or materially modified presenta-tion of the man whom we all know so well.

My own study of him began in Illinois, in the year 1858, before he had attained his national fame or had been thought of as a probable President of the United States. That study at last led me to write and to print in my own journal, in his district, the first editorial nomination of him as the candidate of the Republican party. Not long after his election I was ordered by him to Washington, to wait there for his further instructions and for his arrival. I did so, receiving an appointment on his official staff. After a three months' interval of army service, by his express permission, I was ordered to the White House and placed in sole charge of his correspondence, with such other duties as came to me, from time to time. Here I remained until the Autumn of 1864, when I was promoted to what was then believed to be a higher appointment. A conscious as well as unconscious study of Mr. Lincoln went on during all those years, seeing him and talking with him under every variety of circumstance.

There was in him an intense, absorbing, all-pervading love of truth, of righteousness, of justice, of his fellow men, with a continuously reverent acknowledgment of God and of a strong sense of divine help and leading, which cannot by any rational examiner be separated from a very highly developed Christian attainment.

Mr. Lincoln's years in the White House were years of almost ceaseless heart pain, whereof he at times said that he was slowly dying. To him came thus the fulfillment of the divine annunciation, "Through much tribulation do ye enter the kingdom."

I shall not in this place present any small and impertinent anecdote of personal contact or conversation, not any mere glittering bubble upon a stream which had swollen into a great flood. The flowing of that spiritual tide must be watched as to its continuous power and direction, as it widened and deepened until it passed out and beyond all earthly observation.

It might be well for those who are at all disposed to criticize or distract, to inquire, thoughtfully, how far the recorded Christian testimony of the great President does, or does not, fulfill the word that is final: "On these two commandments, the love of God and the love of the neighbor, depend all the Law and the Prophets." I have seen him, more than once, with a great light on his face, a shining from within that awed and startled me. Right there is an unspeakable solemnity of thought and faith. I will transfer its consideration to those who are able to understand, from their own inner life, a spiritual lamp for that illumination. For all time to come, and especially for all generations of Americans, the life of Abraham Lincoln presents a deep and priceless teaching concerning the reality of that inner birth, growth, development, whose richest treasures are, nevertheless, hidden from all eyes but those of God himself.

WILLIAM O. STODDARD.

Madison, New Jersey,
    March 7, 1913.

ABRAHAM LINCOLN THE CHRISTIAN

EARLY TRAINING

MR. LINCOLN's parents were Christians, first affiliated with the Free-Will Baptist Church in Kentucky, and afterward with the Presbyterian Church in Indiana.[1] Their home was a home of prayer, the Bible was read morning and evening, and his father always returned thanks at the table. On one occasion the only thing they had for dinner was roasted potatoes. After the father had returned thanks for "these blessings," young Abe looked up and said, "Dad, I call these mighty poor blessings."[2]

His mother seems to have been a woman of superior character for her time and surroundings. She had attended a school in Virginia, and was intellectually above those around her. She was especially devoted in her Christian life, striving to live up to the teachings of the Bible, which was her daily companion, and sought to follow the scriptural injunction, "Train up a child in

the way he should go: and when he is old,
he will not depart from it." On Sunday
she would read to her children those Bible
stories so interesting to all children, and
pray with them.[3] She impressed her own
ideals and convictions of righteousness in-
delibly on her son, and her earnest prayers
made a lifelong impression upon his young
mind; for he himself said, after he became
President, speaking of his mother: "I
remember her prayers, and they have always followed me. They have clung to
me all my life."[4]

The opportunities for attending public
worship were very meager. A log meeting-
house had been erected about three miles
from the Lincoln home in Kentucky, where
traveling preachers occasionally held service. Little Abe attended these "meetings"
with his parents. When only five years
old he was so impressed with the preach-
ing, or, perhaps, the manner of the preach-
ing, that on returning home he would get
upon a stool or block of wood and preach
to the other children or the rest of the
family, shouting and pounding the Bible
with his little fist just like the preacher.[5]

MOTHER'S DEATH

When Abe was nine years old his mother died, her death occurring on October 5, 1818. A friend present at the time says: "The mother knew she was going to die, and called her children [Abe and Sarah] to her bedside. She was very weak, and the children leaned over while she gave her last message. Placing her feeble hand on little Abe's head, she told him to be kind and good to his father and sister; to both she said, 'Be good to one another,' expressing a hope that they might live as they had been taught by her, to love their kindred and worship God."[6]

Little did this mother, "dying amid the miserable surroundings of a home in the wilderness," dream that her name, Nancy Hanks Lincoln, was to become immortal through the ragged, barefoot, hapless lad who gazed with wondering eyes upon this strange transition. Earth's noblest crown has been wreathed about her memory, and never more beautifully told than in these words: "Though of lowly birth, the victim of poverty and hard usage, she takes a place in history as the mother of a son who liberated a race of men. At her side stands another mother, whose Son performed a similar service for all mankind eighteen hundred years before."[7]

There was no one to hold religious services when Mrs. Lincoln died, and this added greatly to the little boy's grief. It weighed so heavily upon his young heart that, eight or nine months afterward, having learned to write, his first letter was to a Baptist itinerant preacher whom he had heard in Kentucky, the Rev. David Elkin, asking him to preach a funeral sermon at his mother's grave. The preacher agreed to come, an appointment was made, and the settlers from many miles around gathered in the woods on the hill to hear the funeral sermon at Nancy Lincoln's grave.[8]

The effect of this mother's prayers, teachings, and dying benediction may best be told by her own son, after he became known and loved the wide world over: "All that I am, all that I hope to be, I owe to my angel mother—blessings on her memory."[9] Lincoln never forgot this Christian mother's life and teachings. She inspired him with pure and noble motives.

Her example was one of sweetness and patience. He never forgot her motherly devotion and tenderness and care. "His character was planted in this Christian mother's life. Its roots were fed by this Christian mother's love; and those that have wondered at the truthfulness and earnestness of his mature character have only to remember that the tree was true to the soil from which it sprang."[10] "A great man," says John G. Holland, "never drew his infant life from a purer or more womanly bosom than her own."

Boyhood

About a year after his mother's death young Abe was blessed with a stepmother, whom his father had brought from Kentucky. She was even a stronger character than the first Mrs. Lincoln, and continued the good training and wise teaching so well begun by her predecessor. She was very fond of Abe, and he learned to love her as his own mother. She bears testimony to his goodness in these words, spoken after his death: "Abe was a good boy, and I can say what scarcely one woman—a mother—in a thousand can say: Abe never gave me a cross word or look, and never refused in fact or appearance to do anything I requested of him. I never gave him a cross word in all my life. His mind and mine—what little I had—seemed to run together. He was a dutiful son to me always. I think he loved me truly. I had a son, John, who was raised with Abe. Both were good boys, but I must say, both now being dead, that Abe was the best boy I ever saw, or expect to see."[11] His cousin, Dennis Hanks, also bears similar testimony (June 13, 1865): "Abe was a good boy—an affectionate one—a boy who loved his parents and was obedient to their every wish."[12]

The books to which young Lincoln had access were few, but they were the best. The first was the Bible. He kept it within easy reach, and read it over and over again. He could repeat much of it from memory. His mind was saturated with its precepts and his heart was filled with its truths. The second book which he read was Bunyan's Pilgrim's Progress, which his father borrowed for him. The third, pre-

sented to him by a Mrs. Bruner, was
Æsop's Fables, which he committed to
memory.[13]   Could three better books be
chosen for a boy to-day from the libraries
of the world?   "These three books did
much to perfect that which his mother's
teachings had begun, and to form a character which, for quaint simplicity, earnestness, truthfulness, and purity, has never
been surpassed among the historic per-
sonages of the world."[14]

YOUTH

But little is preserved of Lincoln's youth
to show his religious bent.   With the free-
and-easy life of those pioneer days, it is
doubtful if anyone with Lincoln's buoyant
nature would manifest any special religious
interest.   A few things indicate the better
thought of his youthful mind and the
deeper emotion of his youthful heart.

In his fourteenth year, while at school,
he wrote on the flyleaf of his schoolbook:

> Abraham Lincoln
> his hand and pen—
> he will be good but
> god knows When.

At another time he wrote in a school-mate's (Joseph C. Richardson) copybook:

> Good boys who to their books apply
> Will all be great men by and by.[15]

These show two things: First, that the youthful boy had faith in his mother's God; and, second, that he believed his mother's teachings—that goodness is the first thing to be sought for. As our Master has taught: "Seek ye first the kingdom of God, and his righteousness; and all these things shall be added unto you."

The sacred songs that he most loved indicate something of his religious nature. They were, "Am I a Soldier of the Cross?" "How Tedious and Tasteless the Hours," "There is a Fountain Filled with Blood," and "Alas, and Did My Saviour Bleed?"[16] A soul that can appreciate these hymns must recognize, first, that without the shedding of blood there is no remission of sin; second, that Jesus Christ died upon the cross for the salvation of the world; third, that life without the Saviour is an empty bubble; and, fourth, that loyal devotion to the Christ and His cause is man's highest calling, and the test of true character.

SUPERSTITION

The claim that there was more or less of superstition in his nature, and that he was greatly affected by his dreams, is not to be disputed. Many devout Christians to-day are equally superstitious, and, also, are greatly affected by their dreams. Lincoln grew in an atmosphere saturated with all kinds of superstitious beliefs. It is not strange that some of it should cling to him all his life, just as it was with Garfield, Blaine, and others.

In 1831, then a young man of twenty-two, Lincoln made his second trip to New Orleans. It was then that he visited a Voodoo fortune teller,[17] that is so important in the eyes of certain people. This, doubtless, was out of mere curiosity, for it was his second visit to a city. This no more indicates a belief in "spiritualism" than does the fact that a few days before he started on this trip he attended an exhibition given by a traveling juggler, and allowed the magician to cook eggs in his low-crowned, broad-rimmed hat.[18]

First Sight of Slavery

Of deeper significance than his visit to a fortune teller was his first sight of the public sale of slaves during his stay in New Orleans. He saw "Negroes in chains, whipped and scourged." Rambling about the city one morning with his companions, they came upon a slave auction. Men, women, and children were treated as brutes, and sold to the highest bidder. The whole scene was revolting to Lincoln, and his soul was stirred to profoundest depths. With a deep feeling of "unconquerable hate" for an institution that made such inhumanity possible, turning away from the awful sight, he said to his companions, "Boys, by the Eternal God, if ever I get a chance to hit that thing [slavery], I'll hit it hard."[19] Does this not indicate that deep in his nature, beneath the rough and wild exterior life of the young pioneer, there was an abiding belief and trust in the power and guidance of God?

Essay on Christianity

In July, 1831, Mr. Lincoln, being twenty-two years of age, went to New Salem, Illinois, a rude hamlet started two years before, to begin life for himself. He had always lived in log houses in the woods. He had never been inside of a college, and had attended school hardly more than twelve months in all. He never lived where there was a church until he went to the Legislature at Vandalia, in December, 1834.

It has been claimed that at New Salem, being "surrounded by a class of people exceedingly liberal in matters of religion," by reading skeptical literature and discussing it in the tavern and the village store, he himself became quite skeptical. Some of his biographers state that he wrote an essay against Christianity, Jesus Christ, and the Bible, which was read and discussed in the village store until his friend and employer (Mr. Samuel Hill) snatched the manuscript from him, tore it in two, and thrust it into the stove. While this statement has never been supported by any credible evidence, it has been too largely accepted, not because it was reasonable, but because there did not seem to be any direct evidence to the contrary. It is most gratifying to all the lovers of Lincoln and of historic truth to find that the exact opposite is true.

One of Mr. Lincoln's early acquaintances after he went to New Salem was Mr. Mentor Graham, a school-teacher of local renown who flourished in and around New Salem from 1829 to 1860. Mr. Lincoln boarded with Mr. Graham for two years, and studied English grammar and surveying under him. Certainly no one had a better opportunity to know Mr. Lincoln's mind. In a letter written March 17, 1874, from Petersburg, Illinois, where he was then living, to Mr. B. F. Irwin, Pleasant Plains, Illinois, and which was published in an article on "Lincoln's Religious Belief," in the Springfield Journal of May 16, 1874, Mr. Graham says:

"In reply to your inquiries, Abraham Lincoln was living at my house at New Salem, going to school, studying English grammar and surveying, in the year 1833. One morning he said to me, 'Graham,

what do you think about the anger of the
Lord?' I replied, 'I believe the Lord
never was angry or mad and never would
be; that His loving-kindness endureth forever; that He never changes.' Said Lincoln, 'I have a little manuscript written,
which I will show you,' and stated he
thought of having it published. The size
of the manuscript was about one half
quire of foolscap, written in a very plain
hand, on the subject of Christianity, and a
defense of universal salvation. The commencement of it was something respecting
the God of the universe ever being excited,
mad, or angry. I had the manuscript in
my possession some week or ten days. I
have read many books on the subject of
theology, and I don't think, in point of
perspicuity and plainness of reasoning, I
ever read one to surpass it. I remember
well his argument. He took the passage,
'As in Adam all die, even so in Christ shall
all be made alive,' and followed with the
proposition that whatever the breach or
injury of Adam's transgression to the
human race was, which no doubt was very
great, was made just and right by the atone-

ment of Christ. As to Major Hill burning the manuscript, I don't believe he did, nor do I think he would have done such a thing. About the burning of a paper by Hill, I have some recollection of his snatching a letter from Lincoln and putting it into the fire. It was a letter written by Hill to McNamar. His real name was Neil.[20] Some of the school children had picked up the letter and handed it to Lincoln. Neil and Lincoln were talking about it, when Hill snatched the letter from Lincoln and put it into the fire. The letter was respecting a young lady, Miss Ann Rutledge, for whom all three of these gentlemen seemed to have respect."[21]

This is not hearsay, but an authentic and original statement by one whose personal knowledge, character, learning, and standing make him a competent and trustworthy witness. It ought forever to end the base slander that Mr. Lincoln "hurled his wit and keen logic against the sacred teachings of his mother's Bible." What he really did was to make a protest against the "rude theology" of uneducated preachers and the misrepresentations of biblical doctrines by skeptics.

Indications of Religious Belief

At this time, beneath the rough exterior, there was a religious nature and the rudiments of Christian faith, as shown in expressions found in authentic letters and speeches. In 1836 he shows his faith in a ruling Providence in the following words, spoken in a discussion of the question of "woman's rights" and "temperance": "All such questions must first find lodgment with the most enlightened souls who stamp them with their approval. In God's own time they will be organized into law and thus woven into the fabric of our institutions."[22]

December 13, 1836, in a letter to Miss Mary Owens, written while he was in the Legislature, he says, "They will smile as complacently at the angry snarl of the contending Van Buren candidates and their respective friends as the Christian does at Satan's rage."*

In a speech before the Illinois Legislature in January, 1837, speaking of the scenes of the Revolution, he says, "In history, we hope, they will be read of, and recounted, so long as the Bible shall be read." In his closing words he refers to the greatness of the church, saying, "Upon these let the proud fabric of freedom rest, as the rock of its basis, and as truly as has been said of the only greater institution, 'the gates of hell shall not prevail against it.' "*

LIFE MORE SERIOUS

After his removal to Springfield, in 1837, to engage in the practice of law, he entered a new world, encompassed by new associations. He came into contact with people of culture—with "men of thought and men of action," many of them of exalted character, both in church and state. Books were more accessible, and his range of reading increased. Life became more real and serious, and his mind began to seek a true conception of the great principles of life. His regular attendance at church enabled him to hear able and educated ministers who were instructive, suggestive, and eloquent.

HEARD THE REV. PETER AKERS, D.D.

In 1837, then twenty-eight years old, he went with some friends to a camp meet-

ing six miles west of Springfield, at the
"Salem Church." The Rev. Peter Akers,
D.D., of the Methodist Episcopal Church,
a vigorous and fearless man, preached the
sermon. He spoke of certain prophecies,
and predicted "the downfall of castes, the
end of tyrannies, and the crushing out of
slavery." On the way home they were
earnestly discussing the sermon. Lincoln
said: "It was the most instructive sermon,
and he is the most impressive preacher, I
have ever heard. It is wonderful that God
has given such power to men. I firmly
believe his interpretation of prophecy, so
far as I understand it, and especially about
the breaking down of civil and religious
tyrannies; and, odd as it may seem, I was
deeply impressed that I should be somehow
strangely mixed up with them."[23]

We do not claim that at this time Lincoln
was a man of orthodox belief, but we do
claim that he was a believer in God, and
nominally religious.

THE SOUL'S ALMIGHTY ARCHITECT

In a speech at a political discussion in
the hall of the House of Representatives at

Springfield, Illinois, December, 1839, we find this fervid declaration:

If ever I feel the soul within me elevate and expand to those dimensions not wholly unworthy of its Almighty Architect, it is when I contemplate the cause of my country, deserted by all the world beside, and I standing up boldly and alone and hurling defiance at her victorious oppressors. Here, without contemplating consequences, before High Heaven and in the face of the world, I swear eternal fidelity to the just cause, as I deem it, of the land of my life, my liberty, and my love.*

An Oxford Bible

Returning from a visit to the home of the Speeds in Kentucky, Mr. Lincoln writes to Miss Mary Speed, September 27, 1841. Speaking of the cheerfulness of slaves chained together on the steamboat, he says, "How true it is that 'God tempers the wind to the shorn lamb,' or in other words, that he renders the worst of human conditions tolerable, while he permits the best to be nothing better than tolerable." Again, he says: "Tell your mother that I have not got her 'present' [an Oxford Bible][24] with me, but I intend to read it regularly when I return home. I doubt not that it is

really, as she says, the best cure for the
blues, could one but take it according to
the truth."*

LETTERS TO SPEED

It was in 1841 and 1842 that interesting
letters passed between Lincoln and his
friend, Joshua F. Speed, when both were
filled with forebodings and heart-wrestlings
over love matters. "Lincoln frequently
expressed to Speed his belief that the
Almighty had sent their suffering for a
special purpose."

In a letter to Speed, January 1, 1842,
in regard to Speed's apprehension that he
did not love his "intended" as he should,
Lincoln says, "I adopt this as the last
method I can adopt to aid you, in case
(which God forbid!) you shall need my
aid." And, "Let me, who have some
reason to speak with judgment on such a
subject, beseech you to ascribe it to the
causes I have mentioned, and not to some
false and ruinous suggestion of the Devil."*

In a letter to Speed, February 3, 1842,
in reference to' Speed's anxiety over the
sickness of his sweetheart, as well as his

doubts, Lincoln says: "I almost feel a presentiment that the Almighty has sent your present affliction expressly for that object. . . . Should she, as you fear, be destined to an early grave, it is indeed a great consolation to know that she is so well prepared to meet it. Her religion, which you once disliked so much, I will venture you now prize most highly."*

In a letter to Speed, March 27, 1842, he uses these two sentences: "Enough, dear Lord" and "God be praised for that," showing that his mind was ever turned Godward.

In a letter to Speed, July 4, 1842, after Speed was happily married, he says: "I always was superstitious; I believe God made me one of the instruments of bringing Fanny and you together, which union I have no doubt he had foreordained. Whatever he designs he will do for me yet. 'Stand still and see the salvation of the Lord' is my text just now."*

These utterances do not indicate any real religious conviction, but they do indicate that he believed in a ruling Providence.

LETTER TO GEORGE E. PICKETT

February 22, 1842, in a letter to George E. Pickett, who afterward became the General Pickett who led the famous charge at Gettysburg, Mr. Lincoln says: "I have just told the folks here in Springfield on this 110th anniversary of the birth of him whose name, mightiest in the cause of civil liberty, still mightiest in the cause of moral reformation, we mention in solemn awe, in naked, deathless splendor, that the one victory we can ever call complete will be that one which proclaims that there is not one slave or one drunkard on the face of God's green earth. Recruit for this victory."*

PEW IN FIRST PRESBYTERIAN CHURCH

After Lincoln's marriage, November 4, 1842, he and his wife took a pew in the First Presbyterian Church of Springfield, Illinois, retaining it until their removal to Washington,[25] except the few years they attended the Episcopal Church.

DENIES CHARGE OF INFIDELITY

MR. THOMAS MOSTILLER, of Menard County, Illinois, in a letter to Mr. B. F.

Irwin, Pleasant Plains, Illinois, April 28, 1874, says: "In regard to your inquiry, just received, of what I heard Lincoln say about a charge of infidelity made against him when a candidate for Congress in 1847 or '48, it was this: I was present and heard Josiah Grady ask Lincoln a question or two regarding a charge made against Lincoln of being an infidel, and Lincoln unqualifiedly denied the charge of infidelity, and said, in addition, his parents were Baptists, and brought him up in the belief of the Christian religion as much as anyone, but was sorry to say he had or made no pretensions of religion himself."[26]

Religious Awakening

During the few years prior to 1850, Mr. Lincoln wrestled with doubt and uncertainty. With a sincere mind he vainly sought the true foundations of character upon which he might build his superstructure. In his searchings after truth he now came under the powerful influence of a distinguished preacher, a profound thinker, and a master of the whole philosophy of the Christian evidences. This man was the Rev. James Smith, D.D., who became pastor of the First Presbyterian Church of Springfield, Illinois, the early part of 1849, and continued in Springfield until the spring of 1861, soon after the inauguration of President Lincoln. The Rev. William Bishop, D.D., in an address at Salina, Kansas, February 12, 1897, gave the following account of Dr. Smith and his testimony concerning Mr. Lincoln's religious thoughts and convictions:

"Dr. Smith was a large, stalwart Scotchman with a big brain, a typical Calvinistic theologian, Websterian in appearance and in strength of logical argument, and, when inspired by the theme or occasion, in eloquence overwhelming. Before coming North he had spent most of his ministry in the South, where he was known far and wide as the great preacher at camp meetings, where his voice could be heard by acres of people hanging upon his lips of force and fire. His reputation was still farther extended and enhanced as a controversialist, a thinker, and a learned 'defender of the faith,' by a great debate which he had at Columbus, Mississippi, in the winter of 1839–40, with a celebrated infidel named C. G. Olmstead, who through a committee of infidel gentlemen challenged him to a public discussion. The discomfiture of this champion of infidelity was inevitable. By the universal testimony, it was a Lilliputian combatant in the hands of a Brobdingnagian antagonist. The substance of this debate, by popular demand, was published, reconstructed and enlarged, in 1843, in a book of two volumes of over six hundred pages, with the title The Christian's Defence.

"Why I have mentioned Dr. Smith and his book so particularly will immediately appear. And I might say, parenthetically, the Doctor presented me with a copy of his book. Perhaps he thought I was skeptical! It has been in my library forty years, and I am thinking of donating it to the Kansas State Historical Society, as a historic memento of the man and the book, that under divine guidance, converted Lincoln to the Christian faith. But to resume the narration: I first met Dr. Smith in the summer of 1850 in Jacksonville, at the commencement exercises of Illinois College, from which I had graduated and had just been appointed a member of the faculty of instruction. The acquaintance then formed ripened into mutual and congenial friendship. And during the two years of my connection with the college I was frequently a visitor and guest at his house in Springfield, and when, by reason of removal to another institution in another State, the visits were fewer and farther between, 'a free epistolary correspondence' continued to strengthen and brighten the links of fellowship. With his other accomplishments, Dr. Smith was an interesting and instructive conversational-ist—in fact, quite a raconteur, somewhat like his friend Lincoln, always ready with a story to illustrate his opinions, and which gave piquancy to his conversation. Whenever he had occasion to speak of Lincoln he always evinced the strongest attachment and the warmest friendship for him, which was known to be fully reciprocated. Democrat as he was, and tinged with Southern hues—though never a secessionist—there seemed to be a mystic cord uniting the minister and the lawyer. This was subsequently beautifully shown on the part of Mr. Lincoln, who never forgot to do a generous thing. When he was elected President Dr. Smith and wife were getting old, their children all married and gone, except their youngest son, a young man of twenty-three or four years of age. One of Lincoln's first official acts, after his inauguration, was the appointment of this young man to the consulate at Dundee, Scotland. The Doctor, with his wife and son, returned to the land of his birth. The son soon returned to America, and Dr.

Smith himself was appointed consul, which position he retained until his death in 1871.

"In the spring of 1857 Dr. Smith, anticipating a necessary absence from his church of two or three months during the summer, invited me to supply his pulpit until his return. Being young and inexperienced in the ministry, with considerable hesitation I accepted his urgent invitation. So I spent my college vacation performing as best I could this service. Mr. Lincoln was a regular attendant at church and evidently an attentive hearer and devout worshiper.

"As a college student I had seen and heard him and looked up to him as a being towering above common men; and, I confess, I was not a little intimidated by his presence as he sat at the end of a seat well forward toward the pulpit, with his deep eyes fixed upon me, and his long legs stretched out in the middle aisle to keep them from (using one of his own colloquialisms) being scrouged in the narrow space between the pews. My 'stage fright,' however, was soon very much relieved by his kindliness and words of encouragement.

"On a certain Sunday, the third, as I recollect it, in my term of service, I delivered a discourse on the text, 'Without God in the World.' The straight translation from the Greek is, 'Atheists in the World.' In discussing atheism, theoretical and practical, I endeavored to elucidate and enforce the fallacy of the one and the wickedness of the other. At the close of the service Mr. Lincoln came up and, putting his right hand in mine and his left on my shoulder, with other impressive remarks, said, 'I can say "Amen" to all that you have said this morning.' From that time on my interest in him grew apace.

"He was then known extensively all over the West as a great and good man, and only a year afterward he bounded into national fame by his victory in the great debate with Douglas, who, up to that time, was regarded as a debater invincible.

"During my brief sojourn in Springfield I had many opportunities of meeting Lincoln, hearing him and talking with him at home, in church, in society, and in the courts of justice.

"Dr. Smith returned in due time to resume

his pastoral functions. In reporting to him, in general, my labors in the church as his substitute during his absence, and in particular my conceptions of Lincoln's religious character, he intimated that he knew something of Lincoln's private personal religious experiences, feelings, and beliefs which resulted in his conversion to the Christian faith. After some urging to be more explicit, he made the following statement, which is herewith submitted, couched substantially in his own language. The Doctor said:

" 'I came to Springfield to take the pastoral charge of this church [First Presbyterian] about eight years ago [1849]. During the first of these years, I might say, I had only a speaking or general acquaintance with Mr. Lincoln [now forty years old]. Two or three years previous to my coming here Mrs. Lincoln, who had been a member of our church, for some reason changed her church relations and was a regular attendant at the services of the Episcopal Church. Mr. Lincoln, at that time, having no denominational preferences, went with her. And so the family continued to frequent the sanctuary for a year or more after I began my ministry here. The occasion which opened up the way to my intimate relations to Mr. Lincoln was this, viz.: In the latter part of 1849 death came into his family. His second son died at about three or four years of age. The rector, an excellent clergyman, being temporarily absent, could not be present to conduct the burial service, and I was called to officiate at the funeral. This led me to an intimate acquaintance with the family, and grew into an enduring and confidential friendship between Mr. Lincoln and myself. One result was that the wife and mother returned to her ancestral church, and the husband and father very willingly came with her, and ever since has been a constant attendant upon my ministry. I found him very much depressed and downcast at the death of his son, and without the consolation of the gospel. Up to this time I had heard but little concerning his religious views, and that was to the effect that he was a deist and inclined to skepticism as to the divine origin of the Scriptures, though, unlike most skeptics, he had evi-

dently been a constant reader of the Bible.
I found him an honest and anxious inquirer.
He gradually revealed the state of his
mind and heart, and at last unbosomed his
doubts and struggles and unrest of soul.
In frequent conversations I found that he
was perplexed and unsettled on the funda-
mentals of religion, by speculative difficulties, connected with Providence and
revelation, which lie beyond and above the
legitimate province of religion. With some
suggestions bearing on the right attitude
required for impartial investigation, I placed
in his hands my book (The Christian's
Defence) on the evidence of Christianity,
which gives the arguments for and against
the divine authority and inspiration of the
Holy Scriptures. Mr. Lincoln took the
book, and for a number of weeks, as a
lawyer, examined and weighed the evidence,
pro and con, and judged of the credibility
of the contents of revelation. And while
he was investigating I was praying that
the Spirit of Truth might lead him into
the kingdom of truth. And such was the
result, for at the conclusion of his examina-
tion he came forth his doubts scattered to

the winds and his reason convinced by the arguments in support of the inspired and infallible authority of the Old and New Testaments—a believer in God, in his providential government, in his Son, the way, the truth, and the life, and from that time (nearly seven years) to this day his life has proved the genuineness of his conversion to the Christian faith. For this I humbly ascribe to our heavenly Father the honor and the glory.' "[27]

The preceding declaration by Dr. Smith was made in September, 1857.

LETTER FROM DR. SMITH

In corroboration of this, the Rev. Dr. Smith wrote from Cainno, Scotland, January 24, 1867, to W. H. Herndon, Mr. Lincoln's law partner, as follows: "It was my honor to place before Mr. Lincoln arguments designed to prove the divine authority and inspiration of the Scriptures, accompanied by the arguments of infidel objectors in their own language. To the arguments on both sides Mr. Lincoln gave a most patient, impartial, and searching investigation. To use his own language, he examined the arguments as a lawyer who is anxious to reach the truth investigates testimony. The result was the announcement by himself that the argument in favor of the divine authority and inspiration of the Scriptures was unanswerable."[28]

LETTER FROM MR. NINIAN W. EDWARDS

MR. NINIAN W. EDWARDS, of Springfield, Illinois, a brother-in-law of Mr. Lincoln, wrote to the Rev. James A. Reed on December 24, 1872, as follows: "A short time after the Rev. Dr. Smith became pastor of the First Presbyterian Church in this city Mr. Lincoln said to me, 'I have been reading a work by Dr. Smith on the evidences of Christianity, and have heard him preach and converse on the subject, and I am convinced of the truth of the Christian religion.' "[29]

LETTER FROM MR. THOMAS LEWIS

MR. THOMAS LEWIS was a lawyer, an intimate friend of Mr. Lincoln from 1837 to 1861, and occupied the same law office in Springfield, Illinois. He was an elder in the First Presbyterian Church when Dr.

Smith was the pastor. November 10, 1898, then living in Kansas City, Missouri, he wrote a letter on "Lincoln's Views of the Bible," which was read before the Old Men's Association of the Y. M. C. A., of which he was president. In this letter he says:

"During the fifties Mr. and Mrs. Lincoln visited her uncle in Kentucky. On their return I called on him. At that time he remarked that 'while at my wife's uncle's I got hold of a book entitled Smith on Infidelity, written by your Dr. Smith' (meaning the Rev. James Smith, D.D., pastor of the First Presbyterian Church). 'I read it about half through, and it has given me different views of the Bible from those I have ever entertained, and I want to get that book and finish reading it. Can you help me to get it?' I replied by saying: 'Yes, I heard the Doctor say a few days since he had sold his last book, and I have no doubt that some who have read it would be willing to part with it for the $5 they had paid for it.' Said he, 'As long as the Doctor has been here, I have not made his acquaintance. I wish you would see him, have him get a book, bring him around, and give me an introduction.' I saw the Doctor. He procured the book. Next day I went with him to Mr. Lincoln's office and gave the introduction. After an hour of pleasant conversation we left. I went out first, the Doctor following. As the Doctor passed out, the door partly closed; he reopened it, and said, 'Mr. Lincoln, if agreeable, I should like to see you in our church some day.' 'Dr. Smith,' said Lincoln, 'I will be there next Sunday.' Mr. and Mrs. Lincoln were in the church, and the following Sunday they were there also.

"I was an elder, trustee, treasurer, collector, superintendent of the Sunday school, and pew-renter. The following Tuesday, after the second Sunday, Mr. Lincoln called on me and inquired if there were any pews to rent in the church. I replied, 'Yes, and a very desirable one, vacated by Governor Madison, who has just left the city.' 'What is the rent?' said he. 'Fifty dollars, payable quarterly.' He handed me $12.50. Said he, 'Put it down to me.' From that date he paid each three months on said pew until he left for Washington;

and from the first Sunday he was there I
have not known of his not occupying that
pew every Sunday he was in the city until
he left. The seat was immediately in front
of mine. The third Sunday his children
came in the Sunday school.

"Shortly thereafter there was a revival
in the church, and Mr. and Mrs. Lincoln,
when he was in the city, attended meeting.
In his absence she was there. They attended not only the regular meetings, but
the inquiry meetings also, and it was the
belief that both would unite with the
church. When the candidates were examined Mr. Lincoln was in Detroit, prose-
cuting a patent right case, a branch of the
profession in which he had acquired an
enviable reputation. Mrs. Lincoln stated
that she was confirmed in the Episcopal
Church when twelve years of age, but
did not wish to join the church by letter,
but upon profession of faith, as she was
never converted until Dr. Smith's preach-
ing. She was admitted [1852]. Mr. Lincoln
never applied. Some months later the session of the church invited Mr. Lincoln to
deliver a lecture on the Bible. When it

became known that Mr. Lincoln was to lecture in the Presbyterian church it assured a full house. It was said by divines and others to be the ablest defense of the Bible ever uttered in that pulpit.

"From the introduction of Mr. Lincoln to Dr. Smith their intimacy was of a most cordial character. At their last meeting previous to Mr. Lincoln's leaving for Washington, as they parted, Mr. Lincoln said, 'Doctor, I wish to be remembered in the prayers of yourself and our church members.' "[30]

This statement by his pastor and confidential friend, corroborated by Mr. Lincoln's brother-in-law and an elder of the church, is an original and authentic source of information, and should forever settle all controversy and cavil touching the religious belief and character of Mr. Lincoln.

Address to Bible Society

About 1850 he accepted an invitation to deliver an address from the pulpit of the First Presbyterian Church before the Springfield Bible Society. "The object of the address was to inculcate the importance

of having the Bible placed in possession of
every family in the State. He closed by
saying: 'It seems to me that nothing short
of infinite wisdom could by any possibility
have devised and given to man this excellent and perfect moral code. It is suited to
men in all conditions of life, and includes
all the duties they owe to their Creator,
to themselves, and to their fellow man.' "31

Message to His Dying Father

January 12, 1851, Lincoln wrote to his
stepbrother, John D. Johnston, concerning
his father, who was very sick, saying:

I sincerely hope father may recover his health,
but, at all events, tell him to remember to call
upon and confide in our great and good and merciful Maker, who will not turn away from him in
any extremity. He notes the fall of a sparrow,
and numbers the hairs of our heads, and He will
not forget the dying man who puts his trust in
Him. Say to him that if we could meet now it
is doubtful whether it would not be more painful
than pleasant, but that if it be his lot to go now,
he will soon have a joyous meeting with many
loved ones gone before, and where the rest of us,
through the help of God, hope ere long to join
them.*

Would you call the author of that letter

to a dying father an infidel, a skeptic, an unbeliever? Who could couch in more beautiful and reverent language the comforting doctrines of the Bible to a dying man?

Befriends a Negro Woman

One afternoon an old Negro woman came into Mr. Lincoln's office and told how her son had gone to New Orleans as a deck hand on a steamboat and had been seized by the police, tried and fined, in accordance with the law then in force concerning free Negroes from other States. He was to be sold to pay his fine and expenses. The governor was appealed to, but regretted that under the law he could do nothing. Greatly agitated, Mr. Lincoln rose to his feet and exclaimed, "By the Almighty! I'll have that Negro back soon, or I'll have twenty years' excitement in Illinois, until the governor does have a legal and constitutional right to do something in the premises."[32]

Eulogy of Henry Clay

Mr. Lincoln delivered a masterly eulogy on Henry Clay in the State House at Springfield, Illinois, July 16, 1852, closing as follows: "Such a man the times have demanded, and such, in the providence of God, was given us. But he is gone. Let us strive to deserve, as far as mortals may, the continued care of Divine Providence, trusting that in future national emergencies He will not fail to provide us the instruments of safety and security."*

Good and Evil

In a speech at Peoria, Illinois, October 16, 1854, in reply to Senator Douglas, he says: "God did not place good and evil before man, telling him to make a choice. On the contrary, He did tell him there was one tree of the fruit of which he should not eat, upon pain of certain death."*

Problem too Mighty

In a letter to George Robertson, August 15, 1855, speaking of the solution of the slavery question, he says, "The problem is too mighty for me—may God, in His mercy, superintend the solution."*

The Battle of Freedom

Mr. Lincoln delivered his first great speech on the right or the wrong of slavery at Bloomington, Illinois, May 29, 1856, before the first Republican State Convention of Illinois. The following extracts give some idea of its lofty Christian tone:

"The battle of freedom is to be fought out on principle. Slavery is a violation of the eternal right. We have temporized with it from the necessities of our condition; but as sure *as God reigns and school children read*, THAT BLACK FOUL LIE CAN NEVER BE CONSECRATED INTO GOD'S HALLOWED TRUTH!"

"Can we as Christian men, and strong and free ourselves, wield the sledge or hold the iron which is to manacle anew an already oppressed race? 'Woe unto them,' it is written, 'that decree unrighteous decrees and that write grievousness which they have prescribed.'"

"Those who deny freedom to others deserve it not themselves, and, under the rule of a just God, cannot long retain it."

Like one inspired, his face aglow, the personification of moral power, he exclaims in closing—

"And while, in all probability, no resort to force will be needed, our moderation and forbearance will stand us in good stead when, if ever, WE MUST MAKE AN APPEAL TO BATTLE AND TO THE GOD OF HOSTS!"[33]

THE PERFECT STANDARD

In his celebrated reply to Douglas, delivered at Chicago, July 10, 1858, Mr. Lincoln speaks thus: "It is said in one of the admonitions of our Lord, 'Be ye (therefore) perfect, even as your Father which is in heaven is perfect.' The Saviour, I suppose, did not expect that any human creature could be as perfect as the Father in heaven; but He said, 'As your Father in heaven is perfect, be ye also perfect.' He set up the standard, and He who did most toward reaching that standard, attained the highest degree of moral perfection."* Lincoln here says "our Lord," and accepts as his standard the perfect character of the Father, and Jesus Christ as our example of "the highest degree of moral perfection."

TRANSGRESSION AND ATONEMENT

MR. ISAAC COGDAL, an intimate friend of Mr. Lincoln from the time he came to Illinois until he went to Washington, in a letter to Mr. B. F. Irwin, April 10, 1874, tells of a conversation he had with Mr. Lincoln in the latter's office in Springfield about 1859, concerning Mr. Lincoln's religious faith. Mr. Herndon was present. He says: "Mr. Lincoln expressed himself in about these words: He did not nor could not believe in the endless punishment of anyone of the human race. He understood punishment for sin to be a Bible doctrine; that the punishment was parental in its object, aim, and design, and intended for the good of the offender; hence it must cease when justice was satisfied. He added that all that was lost by the transgression of Adam was made good by the atonement; all that was lost by the fall was made good by the sacrifice. And he added this remark, that punishment being a provision of the gospel system, he was not sure but the world would be better if a little more punishment was preached by our ministers, and not so much pardon for sin."[34]

Drinks Adam's Ale

May 19, 1860, a committee waited upon Lincoln at his home in Springfield to notify him of his nomination. After his reply he ordered "something to drink." Mr. Lincoln gravely said: "Gentlemen, we must pledge our mutual healths in the most healthy beverage which God has given to man. It is the only beverage I have ever used or allowed in my family, and I cannot conscientiously depart from it on the present occasion—it is pure Adam's ale from the spring."[35]

IMPLORES DIVINE HELP

May 21, 1860, after his nomination, in a letter to J. R. Giddings, he says, "May the Almighty grant that the cause of truth, justice, and humanity shall in no wise suffer at my hands."*

May 23, 1860, in a letter to George Ashmun and the Republican National Convention, he says, "Imploring the assistance of Divine Providence, . . . I am most happy to coöperate for the practical success of the principles declared by the convention."*

THE BATEMAN INTERVIEW

At the time of Lincoln's nomination and election in 1860, Hon. Newton Bateman was superintendent of public instruction for the State of Illinois. Lincoln often went into his office for a quiet talk. Mr. Bateman tells of one of these "talks" near the close of October, only a few days before the election. Lincoln was very anxious to know how the ministers of Springfield were going to vote. A careful canvass of the city had been made, and each citizen had declared for whom he intended to vote. The list was before Lincoln, and, with Mr. Bateman, he examined it carefully. All but three of the ministers, and a large majority of the church members, were against Lincoln. Drawing forth a pocket New Testament, Lincoln said, "I am not a Christian—God knows I would be one—but I have carefully read the Bible, and I do not so understand this book." With trembling voice and his cheeks wet with tears, he continued: "I know there is a God, and that He hates injustice and slavery. I see the storm coming, and I know that His hand is in it. If He has a place and work for me—and I think He has—I believe I am ready. I am nothing, but truth is everything. I know I am right, because I know that liberty is right, for Christ teaches it, and Christ is God.   I have told them that 'a house divided against itself cannot stand,' and Christ and reason say the same; and they will find it so. Douglas don't care whether slavery is voted up or down, but God cares, and humanity cares, and I care; and with God's help I shall not fail.   I may not see the end; but it will come, and I shall be vindicated; and these men will find that they have not read their Bibles aright." After a pause, he resumed: "Doesn't it appear strange that men can ignore the moral aspect of this contest?   A revelation could not make it plainer to me that slavery or the government must be destroyed.   The future would be something awful, as I look at it, but for this rock on which I stand [alluding to the Testament which is still held in .his hand], especially with the knowledge of how these ministers are going to vote.   It seems as if God had borne with this thing [slavery] until the very teachers of religion have come to defend it from the Bible, and to claim for it a divine character and sanction; and now the cup of iniquity is full, and the vials of wrath will be poured out."

Mr. Bateman adds: "Everything he said was of a peculiarly deep, tender, and religious tone, and all was tinged with a touching melancholy. . . . After further reference to a belief in the Divine Providence, and the fact of God in history, the conversation turned upon prayer. He freely stated his belief in the duty, privilege, and efficacy of prayer, and intimated in no unmistakable terms that he had sought in that way the divine guidance and favor." As they were about to separate Mr. Bateman remarked: "I have not supposed that you were accustomed to think so much upon this class of subjects. Certainly your friends generally are ignorant of the sentiments you have expressed to me." Lincoln quickly replied, "I know they are; but I think more on these subjects than upon all others, and I have done so for years; and I am willing that *you* should know it."[36]

With this remarkable scene, coupled with the testimony of his pastor, every honest mind must be convinced that Mr. Lincoln had found his way to the Christian standpoint—that he stood on the eternal truth.

In the Garden of Gethsemane

JUDGE JOSEPH GILLESPIE, an old friend living at Edwardsville, Illinois, tells of a conversation he had with Mr. Lincoln in the latter's home in Springfield, Illinois, at the beginning of January, 1861, in which Mr. Lincoln said: "I see the duty devolving upon me. I have read, upon my knees, the story of Gethsemane, where the Son of God prayed in vain that the cup of bitterness might pass from Him. I am in the garden of Gethsemane now, and my cup of bitterness is full and overflowing."

"I then told him," says Judge Gillespie, "that as Christ's prayer was not answered and His crucifixion had redeemed the great part of the world from paganism to Christianity, so the sacrifice demanded of him might be a great beneficence." Mr. Gillespie adds, "Little did I then think how prophetic were my words to be, or what a great sacrifice he was called to make."[37]

May Fall Like Peter

Mr. John G. Nicolay, his private secretary, says that after his election, before he left Springfield for Washington, Mr. Lincoln said to a friend, the Rev. Albert Hale, pastor of the Second Presbyterian Church of Springfield: "Mr. Hale, I have read my Bible some, though not half as much as I ought, and I have always regarded Peter as sincere when he said he would never deny his Master. Yet he did deny Him. Now I think that I shall keep my word and maintain the stand I have taken; but, then, I must remember that I am liable to infirmity, and may fall."[38]

Reliance upon God

FAREWELL ADDRESS

In his good-by speech at Springfield, Illinois, February 11, 1861, the day on which he started for Washington, standing on the rear platform of the car, Mr. Lincoln said:

To-day I leave you. I go to assume a task more difficult than that which devolved upon General Washington. Unless the great God who assisted him shall be with and aid me, I must fail; but if the same Omniscient Mind and Almighty Arm that directed and protected him shall guide and support me, I shall not fail—I shall succeed. Let us all pray that the God of our fathers may not forsake us now. To Him I commend you all. Permit me to ask that with equal sincerity and faith you will invoke His wisdom and guidance for me.[39]

JOURNEY TO WASHINGTON

In his address to the Legislature at Columbus, Ohio, February 13, he said: "I can turn and look for that support without which it will be impossible for me to perform that great task. I turn, then, and look to the American people and to that God who has never forsaken them."*

At Steubenville, Ohio, February 14, he said, "Unless sustained by the American people and God, I cannot hope to be successful."[40]

At Buffalo, New York, February 16, he said: "I am sure I bring a heart true to the work. For the ability to perform it, I must trust in that Supreme Being who has never forsaken this favored land, through the instrumentality of this great and intelligent people. Without that assistance I shall surely fail; with it, I cannot fail."*

To the Legislature at Albany, New York, February 18, he said, "I still have confidence that the Almighty, the Maker of the Universe, will, through the instrumentality of this great and intelligent people, bring us through this as He has through all the other difficulties of our country."*

At the City Hall in New York on February 20 he said, "We look for a restoration of fraternal relations between the States—only to be accomplished by peaceful and conciliatory means, aided by the wisdom of Almighty God."[41]

At Newark, New Jersey, February 21, he said, "I am sure, however, that I have not the ability to do anything unaided of God, and that without His support, and that of this free, happy, prosperous, and intelligent people, no man can succeed in doing that the importance of which we all comprehend."[42]

To the Senate at Trenton, New Jersey, February 21, referring to the Revolutionary War, he said, "I shall be most happy, indeed, if I shall be an humble instrument in the hands of the Almighty, and of this, his most chosen people, as the chosen instrument—also in the hands of the Almighty—for perpetuating the object of that great struggle."[43]

"RATHER BE ASSASSINATED"

He made a remarkable speech at Independence Hall, Philadelphia, on Washington's Birthday. In speaking of the duty of maintaining the rights and liberty of man bequeathed to us by the fathers, under God, he exclaims: "If this country cannot be saved without giving up that principle, I was about to say I would rather be assassinated on the spot than to surrender it. . . . I have said nothing but what I am willing to live by, and, if it be the pleasure of Almighty God, die by."*

First Night in Washington

The first night after his arrival in Washington, February 23, 1861, the Peace Conference called upon him at the Willard Hotel. In answer to a question from William E. Dodge, in reference to his duty, Lincoln said: "With the support of the people and the assistance of the Almighty, I shall undertake to perform it."[44]   A little later, on the same occasion, Lincoln said: "Freedom is the natural condition of the human race, in which the Almighty intended men to live. Those who fight the purpose of the Almighty will not succeed. They always have been, they always will be, beaten."[44]   These utterances show that Lincoln trusted in God and not in himself.

Prays before the Inauguration

"Mrs. Lincoln said that Mr. Lincoln wrote the conclusion of his inaugural address the morning it was delivered. The family being present, he read it to them. He then said he wished to be left alone for a short time. The family retired to an adjoining room, but not so far distant but that the voice of prayer could be distinctly heard. There, closeted with God alone, surrounded by the enemies who were ready to take his life, he commended his country's cause and all dear to him to God's providential care, and with a mind calmed with communion with his Father in heaven, and courage equal to the danger, he came forth from that retirement ready for duty."[45]

First Inaugural Address

In his first inaugural address, March 4, 1861, we find these two sentences, expressing profound faith in God: "If the Almighty Ruler of Nations, with His eternal truth and justice, be on your side of the North, or on yours of the South, that truth and that justice will surely prevail by the judgment of this great tribunal of the American people." And, again, he says, "Intelligence, patriotism, Christianity, and a firm reliance on Him who has never yet forsaken this favored land, are still competent to adjust, in the best way, all our present difficulty."*

His Only Ruler

Shortly after he became President Mrs. Lincoln reported to him that it was rumored that Seward was the power behind the throne. Lincoln very emphatically replied: "I may not rule myself, but certainly Seward shall not. The only ruler is my conscience—following God in it— and these men will have to learn that yet."[46]

First Letter of Condolence

On May 25, 1861, he wrote a letter to the parents of Colonel Ellsworth, of whom he was very fond, regarding his death. He closed by saying, "May God give you that consolation which is beyond all earthly power."*

First Message to Congress

His first message to the Thirty-seventh Congress, July 4, 1861, closes with these words: "And having thus chosen our

course, without guile and with pure purpose, let us renew our trust in God, and go
forward without fear and with manly
hearts."*

REPLY TO TYCOON OF JAPAN

August 1, 1861, in reply to the Tycoon
of Japan, he closes with these words: "I
pray God to have your Majesty always in
his safe and holy keeping."*

FIRST NATIONAL FAST-DAY

That "Mr. Lincoln was profoundly and
intensely religious" is shown in his procla-
mations of days of fasting, prayer, and
thanksgiving. The first proclamation of a
national fast-day was issued August 12,
1861, as follows:

Whereas a joint committee of both houses of
Congress has waited on the President of the United
States and requested him to "recommend a day
of public prayer, humiliation, and fasting, to be
observed by the people of the United States with
religious solemnities and the offering of fervent
supplications to Almighty God for the safety and
welfare of these States, His blessings on their arms,
and a speedy restoration of peace":

And whereas it is fit and becoming in all people,

at all times, to acknowledge and revere the supreme government of God; to bow in humble submission to His chastisements; to confess and deplore their sins and transgressions, in the full conviction that the fear of the Lord is the beginning of wisdom; and to pray with all fervency and contrition for the pardon of their past offences, and for a blessing upon their present and prospective action:

And whereas when our own beloved country, once, by the blessing of God, united, prosperous and happy, is now afflicted with faction and civil war, it is peculiarly fit for us to recognize the hand of God in this terrible visitation, and in sorrowful remembrance of our own faults and crimes as a nation and as individuals, to humble ourselves before Him and to pray for His mercy—to pray that we may be spared farther punishment though most justly deserved; that our arms may be blessed and made effectual for the reëstablishment of law, order, and peace throughout the wide extent of our country; and that the inestimable boon of civil and religious liberty, earned under His guidance and blessing by the labors and sufferings of our fathers, may be restored in all its original excellence:

Therefore, I, Abraham Lincoln, President of the United States, do appoint the last Thursday of September next as a day of humiliation, prayer, and fasting for all the people of the nation. And I do earnestly recommend to all the people, and

especially to all ministers and teachers of religion,
of all denominations, and to all heads of families,
to observe and keep that day, according to their
several creeds and modes of worship, in all humility
and with all religious solemnity, to the end that
the united prayer of the nation may ascend to the
Throne of Grace, and bring down plentiful blessings upon our country.*

First Annual Message to Congress

Mr. Lincoln opens his first regular message to Congress, December 3, 1861, by
expressing gratitude to God, and closes by
expressing reliance on Him, as follows:

"In the midst of unprecedented political
troubles we have cause of great gratitude
to God for unusual good health and most
abundant harvests. . . . The struggle of
to-day is not altogether for to-day—it is
for a vast future also. With a reliance on
Providence all the more firm and earnest,
let us proceed in the great task which
events have devolved upon us."*

Refers Convict to Mercy of God

February 4, 1862, in granting a respite
to Nathaniel Gordon, convicted for being
engaged in the slave trade, he closes with

these words: "In granting this respite it
becomes my painful duty to admonish the
prisoner that, relinquishing all expecta-
tion of pardon by human authority, he
refer himself alone to the mercy of the
common God and Father of all men."*

His Great Sorrow

Thursday, February 20, 1862, Mr. Lincoln experienced what, perhaps, was the greatest sorrow of his life, in the death of his little boy, Willie. He regarded it as an act of Providence, but could not understand it.

"hard to have him die"

One who helped to prepare the body for burial relates the following: "When Willie died, as he lay on the bed, Mr. Lincoln came to the bed, lifted the cover from the face of his child, gazed at it long and earnestly, murmuring: 'My poor boy, he was too good for this earth. God has called him home. I know that he is much better off in heaven, but then we loved him so. It is hard, hard to have him die!' "[47]

A CHRISTIAN NURSE

A Christian lady from Massachusetts, who had come to nurse the children in their sickness, speaks of Lincoln's great

affliction and sadness. On the morning of
the funeral she assured him that many
Christians were praying for him. With
eyes suffused with tears, he replied: "I am
glad to hear that. I want them to pray
for me. I need their prayers." The lady
expressed her sympathy with him as they
were going out to the burial. Thanking
her gently, he said, "I will try to go to
God with my sorrows." She asked him a
few days after if he could not trust God.
With deep religious feeling, he replied: "I
think I can, and I will try. I wish I had
that childlike faith you speak of, and I
trust He will give it to me." Then the
memory of his mother filled his mind with
tenderest recollections, and he said: "I
had a good Christian mother, and her
prayers have followed me thus far through
life."[48]

THE REV. FRANCIS VINTON, D.D.

From this time Lincoln's life was filled
with the deepest sadness and melancholy.
Every Thursday was set apart for the
indulgence of his grief, at which time he
would see no one. Mrs. Lincoln became

alarmed for his health.   Dr. Francis Vinton,
rector of Trinity Church, New York, was
spending a few days in Washington. Being
an acquaintance of Mrs. Lincoln, he was
invited to the White House.   He was
apprised of the President's condition.   A
favorable opportunity presenting itself, Dr.
Vinton spoke to Lincoln about it, and told
him it was sinful to grieve so much over
the departed, and unworthy a believer in
the Christian religion.   The scene which
followed is described as follows:

"Your son," said Dr. Vinton, "is *alive*,
in paradise.   Do you remember that passage in the Gospels, 'God is not a God of
the dead, but of the living: for all live
unto him'?"   As Mr. Lincoln caught the
words, "Your son is alive," he started
from his seat, as one aroused from a
stupor, and exclaimed, "Alive! *Alive!*
Surely you mock me."   "No, sir; believe
me," replied Dr. Vinton; "it is a most
comforting doctrine of the church, founded
upon the words of Christ himself."   Mr.
Lincoln threw his arm around Dr. Vinton's
neck, laid his head upon his breast, and
sobbed aloud, "*Alive? Alive?*"   Dr. Vinton,

greatly moved, said: "My dear sir, believe this, for it is God's most precious truth. Seek not your son among the dead; he is not there; he lives to-day in paradise! Think of the full import of the words I have quoted. The Sadducees, when they questioned Jesus, had no other conception than that Abraham, Isaac, and Jacob were dead and buried. Mark the reply: 'Now that the dead *are* raised, even Moses showed at the bush when he called the Lord the God of Abraham, the God of Isaac, and the God of Jacob. For He is not the God of the dead, but of the living, *for all live unto Him!*' Did not the great patriarch mourn his sons as dead? 'Joseph is not, and Simeon is not, and ye will take Benjamin, also!' But Joseph and Simeon were both living, though he believed it not. Indeed, Joseph being taken from him was the eventual means of the preservation of the whole family. And so God has called your son into His upper kingdom —a kingdom and an existence as real, more real, than your own. It may be that he too, like Joseph, has gone, in God's good providence, to be the salvation of *his* father's household. It is a part of the Lord's plan for the ultimate happiness of you and yours. Doubt it not."

Dr. Vinton told Lincoln that he had a sermon upon the subject. Mr. Lincoln asked him to send it to him as early as possible, and thanked him repeatedly for his cheering and hopeful words. When Lincoln received the sermon he read it over and over, and had a copy made for his own private use. A member of the family said that Mr. Lincoln's views in relation to spiritual things seemed changed from that hour.[49]

Responsibility to God

March 6, 1862, President Lincoln sent to the Senate and House of Representatives a message recommending compensated emancipation of slavery, closing with these words: "In full view of my responsibility to my God and my country, I earnestly beg the attention of Congress and the people to the subject."*

Must Work Out Destiny

In April, 1862, the Rev. N. W. Miner and wife, of Springfield, Illinois, visited the

Lincolns at the White House. Mr. Lincoln
was sad and dejected over the death of little Willie, and the destruction of life at the
battle of Shiloh. He was discouraged. Mr.
Miner said: "Well, Mr. Lincoln, you have
this encouragement: Christian people all
over the country are praying for you as
they never prayed for mortal man before."
"I believe that," he replied, "and this has
been an encouraging thought for me. If I
were not sustained by the prayers of God's
people, I could not endure the constant
pressure. I should give up hoping for
success." Mr. Miner asked, "Do you
think, judging from your standpoint, that
we shall be able to put down the rebellion?"
He answered: "You know I am not of a
very hopeful temperament. I can take
hold of a thing and hold on a good while.
By trusting God for help, and believing
that our cause is just and right, I firmly
believe we shall conquer in the end." After
further conversation he said: "I would
gladly, if I could, take my neck from under
the yoke, and go home with you to Springfield, and live as I used, in peace with my
friends, than to endure this harassing kind

of life. But," with great solemnity he added, "it has pleased Almighty God to place me in my present position, and, looking to Him for wisdom and divine guidance, I must work out my destiny as best I can."[50]

First Proclamation for Thanksgiving

April 10, 1862, Mr. Lincoln issued his first proclamation recommending thanksgiving for victories as follows:

It has pleased Almighty God to vouchsafe signal victories to the land and naval forces engaged in suppressing an internal rebellion, and at the same time to avert from our country the danger of foreign intervention and invasion:

It is therefore recommended to the people of the United States that, at their next weekly assemblages in their accustomed places of public worship which shall occur after notice of this proclamation shall have been received, they especially acknowledge and render thanks to our Heavenly Father for these inestimable blessings; that they then and there implore spiritual consolation in behalf of all who have been brought into affliction by the casualties and calamities of sedition and civil war; and that they reverently invoke the divine guidance for our national counsels, to the end that they may speedily result in the restoration of peace, harmony, and unity throughout our borders, and hasten the establishment of fraternal relations among all the countries of earth.*

REPLY TO EVANGELICAL LUTHERANS

May 6(?), 1862, in reply to a committee from the Evangelical Lutheran General Synod, Mr. Lincoln spoke, in part, as follows:

You all may recollect that in taking up the sword thus forced into our hands, this government appealed to the prayers of the pious and good, and declared that it placed its whole dependence upon the favor of God. I now humbly and reverently, in your presence, reiterate the acknowledgment of that dependence, not doubting that, if it shall please the Divine Being who determines the destinies of nations, this shall remain a united people, and that they will, humbly seeking the Divine guidance, make their prolonged national existence a source of new benefits to themselves and their successors, and to all classes and conditions of mankind.*

SPEECH TO INDIANA REGIMENT

May 15, 1862, in a speech to the 12th Indiana Regiment, Mr. Lincoln closed by saying, "The thanks of the nation will follow you, and may God's blessing rest upon you now and forever."*

His Great Faith

Ex-Senator James F. Wilson, of Iowa, relates an account of a visit which he with several other gentlemen made upon President Lincoln in June, 1862. Slavery and the war situation were freely discussed. Mr. Lincoln sat quietly in his chair, listening to what different ones had to say. After awhile "He arose and stood at his extreme height. Pausing a moment, his right arm outstretched toward the gentleman who had just ceased speaking, his face aglow like the face of a prophet, Mr. Lincoln gave deliberate and emphatic utterance to the religious faith which sustained him in his great trial to which he and the country were subjected. He said:

"My faith is greater than yours. I not only believe that Providence is not unmindful of the struggle in which this nation is engaged, that if we do not do right, God will let us go our own way to ruin; and that if we do right, He will lead us safely out of this wilderness, crown our arms with victory, and restore our dissevered union, as you have expressed your belief; but I also believe He will compel us to do right, in order that He may do these things, not so much because we desire them as that they accord with His plans of dealing with this nation, in the midst of which He means to establish justice. I think that He means that we shall do more than we have yet done in the furtherance of His plans and He will open the way for our doing it. I have felt His hand upon me in great trials and submitted to His guidance, and I trust that as He shall farther open the way, I will be ready to walk therein, relying on His help and trusting in His goodness and wisdom."[51]

On the Lord's Side

One day during the war a minister said in Lincoln's presence that he hoped "the Lord" was "on our side," to which Mr. Lincoln replied, "I am not at all concerned about that, for I know that the Lord is *always* on the side of the *right;* but it is my constant anxiety and prayer that *I* and this *nation* should be on the *Lord's* side."[52]

With emphatic and deep emotion Mr. Lincoln said to a company of clergymen who called to pay their respects to him in the darkest days of the war, "Gentlemen, my hope of success in this struggle rests on that immutable foundation, the justice and the goodness of God; and, when events are very threatening and prospects very dark, I still hope that, in some way which man cannot see, all will be well in the end, because our cause is just and God will be on our side."[53]

"From the day of his election the President was animated by a profound conviction: 'If we do right, God will be with us; and if God is with us, we cannot fail.' "[54]

A Patient Man

In a letter to Reverdy Johnson, July 26, 1862, he says, "I am a patient man— always willing to forgive on the Christian terms of repentance, and also to give ample time for repentance."*

Letter to Count A. de Gasparin

Mr. Lincoln never hesitated to acknowledge his dependence upon God, whether to people of his own or a foreign land. On August 4, 1862, in reply to a letter from Count de Gasparin, one of the warmest friends of the United States in Europe, who had written to the President concerning the state of the country, Mr. Lincoln said, "I can only say that I have acted upon my best convictions, without selfishness or malice, and that by the help of God I shall continue to do so."*

WRESTLING IN PRAYER

BATTLE OF BULL RUN

About September 1, 1862, after the second defeat of Bull Run, Mr. Lincoln, greatly distressed on account of the number of killed and wounded, said to a lady friend: "I have done the best I could. I have asked God to guide me, and now I must leave the result with Him."[55]

VISIT TO HENRY WARD BEECHER

"Following the disaster of Bull Run, when the strength and resources of the nation seemed to have been wasted, the hopes of the North were at their lowest ebb, and Mr. Lincoln was well-nigh overwhelmed with the awful responsibility of guiding the nation in its life struggle. Henry Ward Beecher, of Brooklyn, was, perhaps, more prominently associated with the cause of the North at that time than any other minister of the gospel. He had preached and lectured and fought its battles in pulpit and press all over the country, had ransomed slaves from his pulpit, and his convictions and feelings were everywhere known.

"Late one evening a stranger called at his home and asked to see him. Mr. Beecher was working alone in his study, as was his custom, and this stranger refused to send up his name, and came muffled in a military cloak which completely hid his face. Mrs. Beecher's suspicions were aroused, and she was very unwilling that he should have the interview which he requested, especially as Mr. Beecher's life had been frequently threatened by sympathizers with the South. The latter, however, insisted that his visitor be shown up. Accordingly, the stranger entered, the doors were shut, and for hours the wife below could hear their voices and their footsteps as they paced back and forth. Finally, toward midnight, the mysterious visitor went out, still muffled in his cloak, so that it was impossible to gain any idea of his features.

"The years went by, the war was finished, the President had suffered martyrdom at his post, and it was not until shortly before Mr. Beecher's death, over twenty years later, that he made known that the mysterious stranger who had called on that stormy night was Abraham Lincoln. The stress and strain of those days and nights of struggle, with all the responsibilities and sorrows of a nation fighting for its life resting upon him, had broken his strength, and for a time undermined his courage. He had traveled alone in disguise and at night from Washington to Brooklyn, to gain the sympathy and help of one whom he knew as a man of God, engaged in the same great battle in which he was the leader. Alone for hours that night, like Jacob of old, the two had wrestled together in prayer with the God of battles and the Watcher over the right until they had received the help which He had promised to those that seek His aid."

The story of this most remarkable incident was first given to the public by Mr. Samuel Scoville, Jr., of Philadelphia, a grandson of Henry Ward Beecher, who heard it from Mrs. Beecher herself.[56]

Preliminary Proclamation

will do god's will.

On the 13th of September, 1862, a delegation of Chicago ministers, representing all religious denominations, called upon President Lincoln to urge him to issue a Proclamation of Emancipation.

In his reply Mr. Lincoln began by saying: "The subject presented in the memorial is one upon which I have thought much for weeks past, and I may even say for months. I am approached with the most opposite opinions and advice, and that by religious men who are equally certain that they represent the divine will. I am sure that either the one or the other class is mistaken in their belief, and perhaps in some respects both. I hope it will not be irreverent for me to say that if it is probable that God would reveal His will to others on a point so connected with my duty, it might be supposed He would reveal it directly to me; for, unless I am more deceived in myself than I often am, it is my earnest desire to know the will of Providence in this matter. And if I can learn what it is, I will do it." After a lengthy discussion of the subject, he said in closing, "I can assure you that the subject is on my mind, by day and night, more than any other. Whatever shall appear to be God's will I will do."*

HIS MIND MADE UP

The lady who was staying at the White House as a nurse says: "Riding down from the Soldiers' Home, or the President's summer residence, he told me of the struggle he had in his mind, and had succeeded, in regard to emancipating so many of that despised race, the blacks, and, said he, 'I have made up my mind with God's help to set them free, for the time has come, and there will never be a better time than now, and I will do the best I can, trusting in God.' "57

COVENANT WITH GOD

Mr. Frank B. Carpenter, the artist, says that Secretary Chase told him that immediately after the battle of Antietam,

September 17, and just before the issue of the preliminary proclamation, Mr. Lincoln called a meeting of his Cabinet, on September 22, 1862, to consider the issuing of his Emancipation Proclamation. He began by saying: "The time for the annunciation of the emancipation policy can be no longer delayed. Public sentiment will sustain it, many of my warmest friends and supporters demand it, *and I have promised my God that I will do it.*" This last was said in a low and reverent tone. Secretary Chase asked if he correctly understood the last sentence. Mr. Lincoln replied: "*I made a solemn vow before God, that if General Lee were driven back from Pennsylvania, I would crown the result by the declaration of freedom to the slaves.*"[58]

NO MISTAKE

September 24, 1862, two days after the preliminary proclamation, a large body of men assembled before the White House to serenade the President. Alluding to the proclamation, Mr. Lincoln said: "What I did, I did after a very full deliberation, and under a heavy and solemn sense of responsibility. I can only trust in God I have made no mistake."*

REPLY TO QUAKERS

September 28(?), 1862, in reply to an address from the Society of Friends delivered to him at the White House by a deputation headed by Mrs. Eliza P. Gurney, Mr. Lincoln said:

I am glad of this interview, and glad to know that I have your sympathy and prayers. We are indeed going through a great trial—a fiery trial. In the very responsible position in which I happen to be placed, being a humble instrument in the hands of our Heavenly Father, as I am, and as we all are, to work out His great purposes, I have desired that all my works and acts may be according to His will, and that it might be so, I have sought His aid; but if, after endeavoring to do my best in the light which He affords me, I find my efforts fail, I must believe that for some purpose unknown to me, He wills it otherwise. If I had had my way, this war would never have been commenced. If I had been allowed my way, this war would have been ended before this; but we find it still continues, and we must believe that He permits it for some wise purpose of His own, mysterious and unknown to us; and though with our limited understandings we may not be

able to comprehend it, yet we cannot but believe
that He who made the world still governs it.*

A Meditation on the Divine Will

September 30(?), 1862, "when everything looked dark and the future of this
nation was uncertain; when men were
wrangling about methods of conducting the
war, and jealousy was rife in the army,
Mr. Lincoln wrote the following medita-
tion. It was not for men, but it was the
expression of a great soul trying to bring
himself into perfect harmony with the
divine":

The will of God prevails. In great contests
each party claims to act in accordance with the
will of God. Both may be, and one must be,
wrong. God cannot be for and against the same
thing at the same time. In the present civil war
it is quite possible that God's purpose is something
different from the purpose of either party; and
yet the human instrumentalities, working just as
they do, are of the best adaptation to effect His
purpose. I am almost ready to say this is probably true; that God wills this contest, and wills
that it shall not end yet. By His mere great power
on the minds of the now contestants, he could have
either saved or destroyed the Union without a
human contest. Yet the contest began. And,

having begun, He could give the final victory to either side any day. Yet the contest proceeds.*

Lincoln and the Sabbath

On November 15, 1862, President Lincoln shows his deepening religious conviction, and his comprehensive faith in the fact that God rules in the affairs of nations as well as of individuals, by his famous "Sunday Rest Order":

The President, Commander-in-chief of the Army and Navy, desires and enjoins the orderly observance of the Sabbath by the officers and men in the military and naval service. The importance for man and beast of the prescribed weekly rest, the sacred rights of Christian soldiers and sailors, a becoming deference to the best sentiments of a Christian people, and a due regard for the Divine Will, demand that Sunday labor in the army and navy be reduced to the measure of strict necessity.

The discipline and character of the national forces should not suffer, nor the cause they defend be imperiled by the profanation of the day or name of the Most High. "At this time of public distress"—adopting the words of Washington in 1776—"men may find enough to do in the service of God and their Country without abandoning themselves to vice and immorality." The first general order issued by the Father of his Country, after the Declaration of Independence, indicates the spirit in

which our institutions were founded and should ever
be defended: "The General hopes and trusts that
every officer and man will endeavor to live and
act as becomes a Christian soldier defending the
dearest rights and liberties of his country."*

SECOND ANNUAL MESSAGE TO CONGRESS

In his annual message to Congress, December 1, 1862, he begins by saying:

While it has not pleased the Almighty to bless
us with a return of peace, we can but press on,
guided by the best light He gives us, trusting that
in His own good time and wise way all will be well.

After discussing the proposed proclamation of emancipation, he said in closing:

We know how to save the Union. The world
knows we do know how to save it. We—even we
here—hold the power and bear the responsibility.
In giving freedom to the slave, we assure freedom
to the free—honorable alike in what we give and
what we preserve. We shall nobly save or meanly
lose the last, best hope of earth. Other means
may succeed; this could not fail. The way is
plain, peaceful, generous, just—a way which, if
followed, the world will forever applaud and God
must forever bless.*

CONTROL OF A HIGHER POWER

In the last days of 1862, when Mr. Lincoln was seriously contemplating issuing

the Emancipation Proclamation, the Rev.
Byron Sunderland, D.D., pastor of the
First Presbyterian Church of Washington,
D. C., which Mr. Lincoln sometimes attended, went with some friends of the
President to call upon him. In a letter
to Rev. J. A. Reed, November 15, 1872,
Dr. Sunderland says that the President
spoke for a half hour and poured forth a
volume of the deepest Christian philosophy
he ever heard. He began by saying:

The ways of God are mysterious and profound
beyond all comprehension—'Who by searching can
find Him out?' Now, judging after the manner
of men, taking counsel of our sympathies and
feelings, if it had been left to us to determine it,
we would have had no war. And, going further
back to the occasion of it, we would have had no
slavery. And, tracing it still further back, we
would have had no evil. There is the mystery
of the universe which no man can solve, and it
is at that point that the human understanding
backs down. And there is nothing left but for
the heart of man to take up faith and believe and
trust where it cannot reason. Now, I believe we
are all agents and instruments of Divine Providence.
On both sides we are working out the will of God.
Yet how strange the spectacle! Here is one half
of the nation prostrated in prayer that God will

help them to destroy the Union and build up a
government upon the corner stone of human bondage. And here is the other half equally earnest
in their prayers and efforts to defeat a purpose
which they regard as so repugnant to their ideas
of human nature and the rights of society, as well
as liberty and independence. They want slavery;
we want freedom. They want a servile class; we
want to make equality practical as far as possible.
And they are Christians and we are Christians.
They and we are praying and fighting for results
exactly the opposite. What must God think of
such a posture of affairs? There is but one solution—self-deception. Somewhere there is a fearful
heresy in our religion, and I cannot think it lies
in the love of liberty and in the aspirations of the
human soul.

What I am to do in the present emergency time
will determine. I hold myself in my present position and with the authority vested in me as an
instrument of Providence. I have my own views
and purposes, I have my convictions of duty, and
my notions of what is right to be done. But I
am conscious every moment that all I am and all
I have is subject to the control of a Higher Power,
and that Power can use me or not use me in any
manner, and at any time, as in His wisdom and
might may be pleasing to Him.

Nevertheless, I am no fatalist. I believe in the
supremacy of the human conscience, and that men
are responsible beings; that God has a right to

hold them, and will hold them, to a strict personal account for the deeds done in the body. But, sirs, I do not mean to give you a lecture upon the doctrines of the Christian religion. These are simply with me the convictions and realities of great and vital truths, the power and demonstration of which I see now in the light of this our national struggle as I have never seen before. God only knows the issue of this business. He has destroyed nations from the map of history for their sins. Nevertheless, my hopes prevail generally above my fears for our Republic. The times are dark, the spirits of ruin are abroad in all their power, and the mercy of God alone can save us.[59]

"Let this Cup Pass"

Mr. Henry C. Whitney, in his Life on the Circuit with Lincoln, says that Mr. Lincoln told Governor Edward Stanley, military governor of North Carolina, that "He earnestly and ofttimes prayed to God in these identical words: 'Father, if it be possible, let this cup pass from me'; but in vain. Therefore he issued the Emancipation Proclamation."[60]

Emancipation Proclamation

The Emancipation Proclamation, which was given to the world January 1, 1863, closed with this prayer: "And upon this act, sincerely believed to be an act of justice, warranted by the Constitution, upon military necessity, I invoke the considerate judgment of mankind, and the gracious favor of the Almighty God."*

WORTHY OF JESUS CHRIST

DR. DAVID GREGG says: "That was an act worthy of Jesus Christ. It was the act of Jesus Christ; for it was the Spirit of Jesus Christ that filled the man with power, and that found an outlet in American history through the personality and pen of Abraham Lincoln."

GRACIOUS FAVOR OF GOD

January 5, 1863, in reply to a letter, Mr. Lincoln wrote the following:

It is most cheering and encouraging for me that in the efforts which I have made and am making for the restoration of a righteous peace for our country, I am upheld and sustained by the good wishes and prayers of God's people. No one is more deeply than myself aware that without His favor our highest wisdom is but as foolishness and that our most strenuous efforts would avail nothing in the shadow of His displeasure.

I am conscious of no desire for my country's welfare that is not in consonance with His will, and no plan upon which we may not ask His blessing. It seems to me that if there be one subject upon which all good men may unitedly agree, it is imploring the gracious favor of the God of Nations upon the struggles our people are making for the preservation of their precious birthright of civil and religious liberty.*

THE VOICE OF GOD

In 1900, the only living one of seven gentlemen who called to congratulate Mr. Lincoln on the success of our arms after he had signed the Emancipation Proclamation, stated that Mr. Lincoln replied as follows: "It is a great satisfaction to me to feel that I have the support of the people in the great struggle to save the Nation's life. I never believed in slavery, but I felt I was elected President of both the North and the South. When Sumter was fired upon, and I called for seventy-five thousand men, my determined purpose was to save the country and slavery, and I called for over half a million men with the same determination. But," said he slowly and with great emphasis, "on many a defeated field there was a voice louder than the thundering of cannon. It was the voice of God, crying, 'Let my people go.' We were all very slow in realizing it was God's voice, but after many humiliating defeats the nation came to believe it as a great and solemn command. Great multitudes begged and prayed that I might answer God's voice by signing the Emancipation Proclamation, and I did it, believing we never should be successful in the great struggle unless we obeyed the Lord's command. Since that the 'God of Battles' has been on our side."[61]

LETTER TO THE REV. ALEXANDER REED

February 22, 1863, in a letter to the Rev. Alexander Reed, superintendent of the United States Christian Commission, who invited Mr. Lincoln to preside at a meeting in the House of Representatives on that day, he said: "Whatever shall be sincerely, and in God's name, devised for the good of the soldier and seaman in their hard spheres of duty, can scarcely fail to be blest. . . . The birthday of Washington and the Christian Sabbath coinciding this year and suggesting together the highest interests of this life and of that to come, is most propitious for the meeting proposed."*

SECOND NATIONAL FAST-DAY

March 30, 1863, President Lincoln issued a proclamation appointing another national fast-day. It reads like the deliverance of one of the ancient prophets, as follows:

Whereas, the Senate of the United States, devoutly recognizing the supreme authority and just government of Almighty God in all the affairs of men and of nations, has by a resolution requested the President to designate and set apart a day for national prayer and humiliation:

And whereas, it is the duty of nations as well as of men to own their dependence upon the overruling power of God; to confess their sins and transgressions in humble sorrow, yet with assured hope that genuine repentance will lead to mercy and pardon; and to recognize the sublime truth, announced in the Holy Scriptures and proven by all history, that those nations only are blessed whose God is the Lord:

And insomuch as we know that by His divine law nations, like individuals, are subject to punishments and chastisements in this world, and may we not justly fear that the awful calamity of civil war which now desolates the land may be but a punishment inflicted upon us for our presumptuous sins, to the needful end of our national reformation as a whole people? We have been the recipients of the choicest bounties of Heaven. We have been preserved these many years in peace and prosperity. We have grown in numbers, wealth, and power as no other nation has ever grown; but we have forgotten God. We have forgotten the gracious hand which preserved us in peace, and multiplied and enriched and strengthened us; and we have vainly imagined, in the deceitfulness of our hearts, that all these blessings were produced by some superior wisdom and virtue of our own. Intoxicated with unbroken success, we have become too self-sufficient to feel the necessity of redeeming and preserving grace, too proud to pray to the God who made us:

It behooves us, then, to humble ourselves before the offended Power, and confess our national sins, and to pray for clemency and forgiveness:

Now, therefore, in compliance with the request and fully concurring in the views of the Senate. I do by this my proclamation designate and set apart Thursday, the 30th day of April, 1863, as a day of national humiliation, fasting, and prayer. And I do hereby request all the people to abstain on that day from their ordinary secular pursuits, and to unite at their several places of public worship and their respective homes in keeping the day holy to the Lord, and devoted to the humble discharge of the religious duties proper to that solemn occasion. All this being done in sincerity and truth, let us then rest humbly in the hope authorized by divine teachings, that the united cry of the nation will be heard on high, and answered with blessings no less than the pardon of our national sins, and the restoration of our now divided and suffering country to its former happy condition of unity and peace.*

REPLY TO PRESBYTERIANS

May 30(?), 1863, a committee of sixty-five members of the General Assembly of the Presbyterian Church in the United States of America, that met in Philadelphia, visited the President, presenting him with resolutions of indorsement and encouragement. In his reply, Mr. Lincoln said:

Relying, as I do, upon Almighty Power, and encouraged, as I am, by the resolutions which you have just read, with the support which I receive from Christian men, I shall not hesitate to use all the means at my control to secure the termination of this rebellion, and will hope for success.*

"GOD WILL BRING US THROUGH SAFE"

MR. OLIVER S. MUNSELL, April 15, 1893, writes of an interview with Mr. Lincoln at the White House in 1863, about three weeks before the battle of Gettysburg. Mr. Munsell was then president of the Illinois Wesleyan University, at Blooming-ton. Mr. Munsell asked, "Will our coun-try come through safe and live?" Mr. Lincoln replied:

I do not doubt—I never have doubted—that our country would finally come through safe and un-divided. But do not misunderstand me; I do not know how it can be. I do not rely on the patriot-ism of our people, though no people have rallied round their king as ours have rallied round me. I do not trust in the bravery and devotion of the boys in blue; God bless them though! God never gave a prince or conqueror such an army as He has given to me. Nor yet do I rely on the loyalty and skill of our generals; though I believe we have the best generals in the world at the head of our armies. But the God of our fathers, who raised up this country to be the refuge and asylum of the oppressed and downtrodden of all nations, will not let it perish now. I may not live to see it, and [he added after a moment's pause] I do not expect to live to see it, but God will bring us through safe.

"When he finished there was silence that could be felt. I do not often weep at human words, but then my eyes were wet with tears and I felt humbled in the pres-

ence of Mr. Lincoln's sublime faith in 'the
God of Battles.' "[62]

Announcement of Gettysburg Victory

July 4, 1863, announcing news from
Gettysburg, with characteristic reverence
he closed by expressing his desire "That on
this day He whose will, not ours, should
ever be done be everywhere remembered
and reverenced with profoundest gratitude."*

A Praying President

THE BATTLE OF GETTYSBURG

GENERAL JAMES F. RUSLING, of Trenton, New Jersey, relates a significant conversation which he heard on Sunday, July 5, 1863, in the room in Washington where General Sickles lay wounded, just after the great victory at Gettysburg. In reply to a question from General Sickles whether or not the President was anxious about the battle at Gettysburg, Lincoln gravely said, "No, I was not; some of my Cabinet and many others in Washington were, but I had no fears." General Sickles inquired how this was, and seemed curious about it. Mr. Lincoln hesitated, but finally replied: "Well, I will tell you how it was. In the pinch of your campaign up there, when everybody seemed panic-stricken, and nobody could tell what was going to happen, oppressed by the gravity of our affairs, I went to my room one day, and I locked the door, and got down on my knees before Almighty God, and prayed to Him mightily for vic-

A PRAYING PRESIDENT

GEN. JAMES F. RUSLING, of Trenton, N. J., relates a significant conversation which he heard on Sunday, July 5, 1863, in the room in Washington where Gen. Sickles lay wounded, just after the great victory at Gettysburg. In reply to a question from Gen. Sickles whether or not the President was anxious about the battle at Gettysburg, Lincoln gravely said, "No, I was not; some of my cabinet and many others in Washington were, but I had no fears." Gen. Sickles inquired how this was, and seemed curious about it. Mr. Lincoln hesitated, but finally replied: "Well, I will tell you how it was. In the pinch of your campaign up there, when everybody seemed panic-stricken, and nobody could tell what was going to happen, oppressed by the gravity of our affairs, I went to my room one day, and locked the door, and got down on my knees before Almighty God, and prayed to Him mightily for victory at Gettysburg. I told Him that this was His war, and our cause His cause, but we couldn't stand another Fredericksburg or Chancellorsville. And I then and there made a solemn vow to Almighty God, that if He would stand by our boys at Gettysburg, I would stand by Him. And He _did_ stand by you boys, and I _will_ stand by Him. And after that (I don't know how it was, and I can't explain it), soon a sweet comfort crept into my soul that God Almighty had taken the whole business into His own hands and that things would go all right at Gettysburg. And that is why I had no fears about you." Asked concerning Vicksburg, the news of which victory had not yet reached him, he said, "I have been praying for Vicksburg also, and believe our Heavenly Father is going to give us victory there, too." Of course, he did not know that Vicksburg had already surrendered the day before. Gen. Rusling says that Mr. Lincoln spoke "solemnly and pathetically, as if from the depth of his heart," and that his manner was deeply touching.

FACSIMILE OF INDORSEMENT OF STORY OF MR. LINCOLN PRAYING OVER
BATTLE OF GETTYSBURG

The author submitted his MS. to General Rusling and General Sickles, both of whom wrote an indorsement on the margin of the MS., as follows:

"I certify that this statement of a conversation between President Lincoln and General Sickles, in my presence, at Washington, D. C., July 5, 1863, relating to Gettysburg, is correct and true. JAMES F. RUSLING, Trenton, N. J., Feb. 17, 1910."

"I hereby certify that the foregoing statement by General Rusling is true in substance. I know from my intimate acquaintance with President Lincoln that he was a religious man —God-fearing and God-loving ruler. D. E. SICKLES, Major General U. S. Army, Ret'd, New York, Feb. 11, 1911."

tory at Gettysburg. I told Him that this was His war, and our cause His cause, but we couldn't stand another Fredericksburg or Chancellorsville. And I then and there made a solemn vow to Almighty God, that if He would stand by our boys at Gettysburg, I would stand by Him. And He *did* stand by you boys, and I *will* stand by Him. And after that (I don't know how it was, and I can't explain it), soon a sweet comfort crept into my soul that God Almighty had taken the whole business into his own hands and that things would go all right at Gettysburg. And that is why I had no fears about you." Asked concerning Vicksburg, the news of which victory had not yet reached him, he said, "I have been praying for Vicksburg also, and believe our Heavenly Father is going to give us victory there, too." General Rusling says that Mr. Lincoln spoke "solemnly and pathetically, as if from the depth of his heart," and that his manner was deeply touching.[63]

PRAYING FOR VICTORY

A lady friend who was staying at the

White House says that on July 9, 1863, while sitting at the dinner table he could not eat, for he seemed so full of trouble as he said, "The battle of Port Hudson is now going on, and many lives will be sacrificed on both sides, but I have done the best I could, trusting in God, for if they gain this important point, we are lost; and, on the other hand, if we could only gain it we shall have gained much; and I think we shall, for we have a great deal to thank God for, for we have Vicksburg and Gettysburg already." The lady said, "Mr. Lincoln, prayer will do what nothing else will; can you not pray?" "Yes, I will," he replied, and while the tears were dropping from his haggard and worn face he said, "Pray for me," and picked up a Bible and went to his room. "Could all the people of the nation have overheard the earnest petition that went up from that inner chamber as it reached the ears of the nurse, they would have fallen upon their knees with tearful and reverential sympathy." That night he received a dispatch announcing a Union victory. He went directly to his friend's room, his face beaming with joy, saying: "Good news! Good news! Port Hudson is ours! The victory is ours, and God is good." When the lady replied, "Nothing like prayer in times of trouble," Mr. Lincoln said, "Yes, O yes—praise—prayer and praise go together." The lady who related the incident says, "I do believe he was a true Christian, though he had very little confidence in himself."[64]

Ah, that was the secret of his greatness—no confidence in himself, but unbounded confidence in God. Who, knowing these incidents, daresay that Lincoln was a fatalist, and had no faith in prayer?

DRIVEN UPON HIS KNEES

In all the great emergencies of his closing years Mr. Lincoln's reliance upon divine guidance and assistance was often extremely touching. "I have been driven many times upon my knees," he once remarked to a friend, Mr. Henry C. Whitney, "by the overwhelming conviction that I had nowhere else to go. My own wisdom, and that of all about me, seemed insufficient for that day."[65]

KNELT IN PRAYER

A minister of the gospel relates the following: "After visiting schools, and holding meetings with the freed people, and attending to other religious service south of Washington and in that city, I felt that I must attend to manifest duty, and offer a visit in gospel love to our noble President; it was immediately granted, and a quarter past six that evening was fixed as the time. Under deep feeling I went. The President gave us a cordial welcome, and after pleasant, instructive conversation, during which he said, in reference to the freedmen, 'If I have been one of the instruments in liberating this long-suffering, downtrodden people, I thank God for it'—a precious covering spread over us. The good man rested his head upon his hand, and under a precious, gathering influence I knelt in solemn prayer. He knelt close beside me, and I felt that his heart went with every word as utterance was given. I afterward addressed him, and when we arose to go, he shook my hand heartily, and thanked me for the visit."[66]

A PASTORAL CALL

A minister from a little village in Central New York went with his congressman to the White House to call on Mr. Lincoln. After the introduction the congressman withdrew, leaving Mr. Lincoln and the minister alone. The minister said: "I have only come to say that the loyal people are sustaining you and will continue to do so. We are giving you all that we have —the lives of our sons as well as our confidence and our prayers. You must know that no pious father or mother ever kneels in prayer these days without asking God to give you strength and wisdom."

The tears filled Lincoln's eyes as he thanked his visitor and said: "But for those prayers I should have faltered and perhaps failed long ago. Tell every father and mother you know to keep on praying and I will keep on fighting, for I am sure that God is on our side."

As the clergyman started to leave the room, Lincoln held him by the hand and said, "I suppose I may consider this a sort of pastoral call."

"Yes," replied the clergyman.

"Out in our country," continued Lincoln, "when a parson made a pastoral call it was always the custom for the folks to ask him to lead in prayer, and I should like to ask you to pray with me to-day; pray that I may have strength and wisdom." The two men knelt side by side before a settee and the minister offered the most fervent appeal to the Almighty Power that ever fell from his lips. As they rose, Lincoln grasped his visitor's hand and remarked in a satisfied sort of way,

"I feel better."[67]

ASKS BISHOP SIMPSON TO PRAY

"One day, in the darkest time of the war," said Bishop Matthew Simpson to Chaplain (afterward Bishop) C. C. McCabe, "I called to see Mr. Lincoln. We talked long and earnestly about the situation. When I rose to go Mr. Lincoln stepped to the door and turned the key and said: 'Bishop, I feel the need of prayer as never before. Please pray with me.' And so we knelt down in that room together and all through the prayer the President responded most fervently."[68]

REQUESTS MANY TO PRAY FOR HIM

MR. JOHN G. NICOLAY, his private secretary, says: "Mr. Lincoln was a praying man; I know that to be a fact. And I have heard him request people to pray for him. . . . Many a time I have heard Mr. Lincoln ask ministers and Christian women to pray for him."[69]

PRAYS WITH SERVANTS

A Negro clergyman writes of a visit to the colored servants at the White House, in which he says: "In the year 1865, while a chaplain at Freedmen's Village, on Arlington Heights, after the assassination, but three weeks before Mrs. Lincoln left the White House, I dined with the servants employed at the house, some of whom had been engaged in personal attendance upon Mr. Lincoln. My object was really to know more about him whose memory is still dear to me. I asked the servants how Mr. Lincoln treated them. I was told that frequently, late at night, Mr. Lincoln came down stairs to teach them to read, and often took such occasions to draw their thoughts toward the Saviour of all mankind. He also often prayed with them."[70]

DAILY PRAYER

"Mr. Lincoln said that after he went to the White House he kept up the habit of daily prayer."[71]

"As a child, in a dark and stormy night, on a rugged way catches hold of the hand of its father for guidance and support, Lincoln clung by faith to the hand of" his Heavenly Father, "and moved calmly through the gloom."

AMBASSADOR OF CHRIST

He always welcomed the visits of ministers, and regarded their calling as the highest. Once he remarked to Father Chiniquy, "There is nothing as great under heaven as to be an ambassador of Christ."[72]

THE PROVIDENCE OF GOD

It is well known that Mr. Lincoln seldom made even a short speech after he was elected President without referring to the omnipotence and providence of God. On the evening of July 7, 1863, a large number of citizens called at the White House to serenade the President. Mr. Lincoln made a speech of only fifteen sentences, in two of which his faith in God is expressly stated: "Fellow citizens: I am very glad indeed to see you to-night, and yet I will not say I thank you for this call; but I do most sincerely thank Almighty God for the occasion on which you have called." Then, referring to John Adams and Thomas Jefferson, he said, "Precisely fifty years after they put their hands to the paper, it pleased Almighty God to take both from this stage of action."*

SECOND PROCLAMATION FOR THANKSGIVING

Having twice called upon the nation for fasting and prayer, when victories came Mr. Lincoln did not forget to ask the nation to set apart a day for thanksgiving and praise. On July 15, 1863, he issued the following proclamation:

It has pleased Almighty God to hearken to the supplication and prayers of an afflicted people, and to vouchsafe to the army and navy of the United States victories on land and on sea so signal and so effective as to furnish reasonable grounds for augmented confidence that the union of these States will be maintained, their Constitution preserved, and their peace and prosperity permanently restored. But these victories have been accorded not without sacrifice of life, limb, health, and liberty, incurred by brave, loyal, and patriotic citizens. Domestic affliction in every part of the country follows in the train of these fearful bereavements. It is meet and right to recognize and confess the presence of the Almighty Father and the power of his hand equally in these triumphs and in these sorrows.

Now, therefore, be it known that I do set apart Thursday, the 6th day of August next, to be observed as a day of national thanksgiving, praise, and prayer, and I invite the people of the United States to assemble on that occasion in their customary places of worship, and, in the forms approved by their own consciences, render the homage due to the Divine Majesty for the wonderful things He has done in the nation's behalf, and invoke the influence of His Holy Spirit to subdue the anger which has produced and so long sustained a needless and cruel rebellion, to change the hearts of the insurgents, to guide the counsels of the government with wisdom adequate to so great a national emergency, and to visit with tender care and consolation throughout the length and breadth of our land all those who, through the vicissitudes of marches, voyages, battles, and sieges, have been brought to suffer in· mind, body, or estate, and finally to lead the whole nation through the paths of repentance and submission to the Divine Will back to the perfect enjoyment of union and fraternal peace.*

First Annual Thanksgiving Day

Although special thanksgiving days have been observed at different times since the days of Plymouth Rock, our modern annual Thanksgiving Day really originated with President Lincoln. His proclamation for the first regular Thanksgiving Day was issued October 3, 1863, as follows. After reciting the blessing that God had bestowed upon the nation, he continues:

No human counsel hath devised, nor hath any mortal hand worked out these great things. They are the gracious gifts of the Most High God, who, while dealing with us in anger for our sins, hath nevertheless remembered mercy.

It has seemed to me fit and proper that they should be solemnly, reverently, and gratefully acknowledged as with one heart and one voice by the American people. I do, therefore, invite my fellow citizens in every part of the United States, and also those who are at sea and those who are sojourning in foreign lands, to set apart and observe the last Thursday of November next as a day of thanksgiving and praise to our beneficent Father who dwelleth in the heavens. And I recommend to them that, while offering up the ascriptions justly due Him for such singular deliverances and blessings, they do also, with humble penitence for our national perverseness and disobedience, commend to His tender care all those who have become widows, orphans, mourners, or sufferers in the lamentable civil strife in which we are unavoidably engaged, and fervently implore the interposition of the Almighty Hand to heal the wounds of the nation, and to restore it, as soon as may be consistent with the Divine purposes, to the full enjoyment of peace, harmony, tranquillity, and union.*

Dedicated to a Great Task

On November 19, 1863, at the dedication of the battlefield of Gettysburg, President Lincoln closed his speech, "the most sublime piece of literature in the English language," with this memorable sentence:

It is rather for us to be here dedicated to the great task remaining before us—that from these honored dead we take increased devotion to that cause for which they gave the last full measure of devotion; that we here highly resolve that these dead shall not have died in vain; that this nation, under God, shall have a new birth of freedom; and that government of the people, by the people, and for the people shall not perish from the earth.*

Of this speech it has been truly said that "the thought and the language are as majestic as those of the ancient prophets."

Instrument of Providence

Mr. Lincoln regarded himself as only an instrument in the hands of Providence, and took unto himself no credit for freeing the slaves. In 1863, Colonel McKaye, of New York, and Robert Dale Owen returned from North Carolina, where they had been sent to investigate the condition of the freedmen. They were telling Mr.

Lincoln how the colored people regarded him. One old man said in meeting: "Massa Linkum, he eberywhar. He know eberyting. He walk de earf like de Lord." Lincoln was greatly touched, and said, impressively, "It is a momentous thing to be the instrument, under Providence, of the liberation of a race."[73]

Constant Recognition of God

On December 7, 1863, in making announcement of Union success in East Tennessee, he closed as follows: "I recommend that all loyal people do, on receipt of this information, assemble at their places of worship and render special homage and gratitude to Almighty God for His great advancement of the national cause."*

Third Annual Message to Congress

He begins his Annual Message to Congress, December 8, 1863, by saying: "Another year of health, and of sufficiently abundant harvests, has passed. For these, and especially for the improved condition of our national affairs, our renewed and profoundest gratitude to God is due."*

Telegram to General Grant

A telegram to General Grant, December 8, 1863, closes with, "God bless you all!"*

A Pardoning President

The generals in the army were greatly annoyed because Mr. Lincoln pardoned so many of the soldiers who were sentenced to be shot. Speaking of this matter on one occasion, Mr. Lincoln said: "They say that I destroy all discipline and am cruel to the army when I will not let them shoot a soldier now and then. But I cannot see it. If God wanted me to see it, he would let me know, and until he does, I shall go on pardoning and being cruel to the end."[74]

The Rev. Newman Hall, of London, tells of a conversation with an officer of the army, who said that soon after he took command there were twenty-four deserters sentenced by court-martial to be shot. President Lincoln refused to sign the warrants for their execution. The officer went to Washington and urged the President to sign them, saying: "Unless these men are

PRESIDENT LINCOLN'S LAST PHOTOGRAPH
"Anointed and prepared for the sacrifice."—Page 141

Taken April 9, 1865, the day of Lee's surrender. Mr. Lincoln was sharpening a pencil for little Tad, when a photographer asked permission to make a picture.

Reproduced from a photograph in the Lincoln Memorial Collection, Washington, D. C., by the courtesy of the owner, Captain O. H. Oldroyd.

The original negative by Gardner is in the collection of Americana of Frederick H. Meserve, New York City.

FIRST PRESBYTERIAN CHURCH, SPRINGFIELD, ILLINOIS

Photographed in 1888

NEW YORK AVENUE PRESBYTERIAN CHURCH
WASHINGTON, D. C.
In Lincoln's Time

THE

HOLY BIBLE,

CONTAINING

THE OLD AND NEW

TESTAMENTS:

WITH

ARGUMENTS

PREFIXED TO THE DIFFERENT BOOKS,

AND MORAL AND THEOLOGICAL

OBSERVATIONS

ILLUSTRATING EACH CHAPTER;

COMPOSED BY

REVEREND MR OSTERVALD, PROFESSOR OF DIVINITY,

AND ONE OF THE MINISTERS OF THE CHURCH AT NEUFCHATEL IN SWISSERLAND.

TRANSLATED AT THE DESIRE OF, AND RECOMMENDED BY
THE SOCIETY FOR PROPAGATING CHRISTIAN KNOWLEDGE.

PRINTED AND SOLD BY ALL THE BOOKSELLERS IN GREAT BRITAIN.
M.DCC.XCIX.

LINCOLN'S MOTHER'S BIBLE

inside cover and title-page of the Lincoln family Bible, from which his mother
[rea]d to him. It bears the date of 1799. Mr. Lincoln wrote his name in it when about
[seven] years old, shortly after his mother's death. It undoubtedly was carried by the
[Lin]colns from Kentucky to Indiana, and thence to Illinois. Mr. Lincoln used it
[whi]le in the White House. It is now in the Oldroyd Lincoln Memorial Collection, in
[the] house in which Lincoln died, 516 Tenth Street, N. W., Washington, D. C.
[Re]produced from a photo by the courtesy of the owner Captain O. H. Oldroyd.

A Lincoln

Reproduced from photograph furnished the author by Mr. William O. Stoddard,
one of Mr. Lincoln's private secretaries, especially for this book. It is his opinion that
it is the most natural photograph ever taken of Mr. Lincoln. It was taken in 1862.

Mrs. Mary Todd Lincoln
From a Photograph presented by her in 1862, to
William O. Stoddard

Reproduced from photograph furnished the author by Mr. William O. Stoddard, one of Mr. Lincoln's private secretaries, especially for this book. Mrs. Lincoln presented the photograph to Mr. Stoddard. She regarded it the best that she ever had taken.

Rev. JAMES SMITH, D.D.
Photograph furnished by his granddaughter, Miss Jeanette E. Smith

Rev. PHINEAS D. GURLEY, D.D.

made an example of, the army itself is in danger. Mercy to the few is cruelty to the many." Mr. Lincoln replied: "General, there are already too many weeping widows in the United States. For God's sake don't ask me to add to the number, for I won't do it."[75]

"A Cup of Cold Water"

The last week in January, 1864, the Sanitary Commission held a four days' session in Washington, at the conclusion of which between forty and fifty of the ladies went in a body to call upon the President. As related by one of the ladies present, he took each by the hand in the usual perfunctory manner, until it became the turn of a little old Quaker lady from Philadelphia. While he still held her hand, she said to him: "Yes, Friend Abraham, thee needs not think thee stands alone. We are all praying for thee. All our hearts, the hearts of all the people are behind thee, and thee *cannot* fail! The Lord has appointed thee, the Lord will sustain thee, and the people love thee. Yea, as no other man was ever loved before does this people love thee. We are only a few weak women, but we represent many. Take comfort, Friend Abraham, God is with thee. The people are behind thee."

"I know it," replied Mr. Lincoln, the great, soft voice rolling solemnly and sweetly forth from the trembling lips; "I know it. If I did not have that knowledge —it is not hope, it is knowledge, the knowledge that God is sustaining and will sustain me until my appointed work is done—I could not live. If I did not believe that the hearts of loyal people were with me, I could not endure it. My heart would have broken long ago. It is that blessed knowledge and that blessed belief that holds me to my work. This has been a bad day, and I was almost overwhelmed when you came in. You have given a cup of cold water to a very thirsty and grateful man. Ladies, you have done me a great kindness to-day. I knew it before. I knew that good men and women were praying for me, but I was so tired I had almost forgotten. God bless you all!"[76]

ADDRESS TO GENERAL GRANT

In an address to General Grant, March

9, 1864, presenting him with the commission of lieutenant-general, he said, "As the country herein trusts you, so, under God, it will sustain you."*

God Bless the Women

On March 18, 1864, at the close of a fair in the Patent Office at Washington for the benefit of the sick and wounded soldiers of the army, President Lincoln closed his short speech as follows: "But I must say, that if all that has been said by orators and poets since the creation of the world in praise of women were applied to the women of America, it would not do them justice for their conduct during this war. I will close by saying, God bless the women of America!"*

Controlled by Events

In a letter to A. G. Hodges, Frankfort, Kentucky, April 4, 1864, Mr. Lincoln says:

I claim not to have controlled events, but confess plainly that events have controlled me. Now, at the end of three years' struggle, the nation's condition is not what either party, or any man, desired or expected. God alone can claim it. Whither it is tending seems plain. If God now

wills the removal of a great wrong, and wills also
that we of the North, as well as you of the South,
shall pay fairly for our complicity in that wrong,
impartial history will find therein new cause to
attest and revere the justice and goodness of God.*

LETTER TO MRS. HORACE MANN

The next day, April 5, 1864, in answer to
a petition from the children and young
people of Concord, Massachusetts, for the
freeing of all slave children, Mr. Lincoln
wrote to Mrs. Horace Mann, who for-
warded the petition, as follows: "While I
have not the power to grant all they ask,
I trust they will remember that God has,
and that, as it seems, He wills to do it."*

LETTER TO GENERAL GRANT

A letter to General Grant, April 30, 1864,
closes with these words: "And now, with a
brave army and a just cause, may God
sustain you."*

RECOMMENDS THANKSGIVING AND PRAYER

On May 9, 1864, Mr. Lincoln issued a
recommendation for thanksgiving and
prayer, as follows: "Enough is known of
army operations within the last five days

to claim an especial gratitude to God, while what remains undone demands our most sincere prayers to, and reliance upon, Him without whom all human effort is vain. I recommend that all patriots, at their homes, in their places of public worship, and wherever they may be, unite in common thanksgiving and prayer to Almighty God."*

GRATEFUL TO ALMIGHTY GOD

In a speech on May 9, 1864, after the Battle of the Wilderness, in response to a serenade at the White House, Mr. Lincoln said, "While we are grateful to all the brave men and officers for the events of the past few days, we should, above all, be very grateful to Almighty God, who gives us victory."*

GOD BLESS THE METHODIST CHURCH

May 18, 1864, in a letter of reply to a deputation of ministers who presented to him resolutions adopted by the Methodist General Conference, he said, "God bless the Methodist Church—bless all the churches—and blessed be God, who, in this our great trial giveth us the churches."*

REPLY TO BAPTISTS

In a letter to a committee consisting of the Rev. Dr. Ide, Honorable J. R. Doolittle, and Honorable A. Hubbell, May 30, 1864, Mr. Lincoln says:

In response to the preamble and resolutions of the American Baptist Home Mission Society, which you did me the honor to present, I can only thank you for thus adding to the effective and almost unanimous support which the Christian communities are so zealously giving to the country, and to liberty. Indeed, it is difficult to conceive how it could be otherwise with anyone professing Christianity, or even having ordinary perceptions of right and wrong. To read in the Bible, as the word of God Himself, that "In the sweat of *thy* face shalt thou eat bread," and to preach therefrom that, "In the sweat of *other men's* faces shalt thou eat bread," to my mind can scarcely be reconciled with honest sincerity. When brought to my final reckoning may I have to answer for robbing no man of his goods; yet more tolerable even this, than for robbing one of himself and all that was his. When, a year or two ago, those professedly holy men of the South met in the semblance of prayer and devotion, and, in the name of Him who said, "As ye would all men should do unto

you, do ye even so unto them," appealed to the
Christian world to aid them in doing to a whole
race of men as they would have no man do unto
themselves, to my thinking they contemned and
insulted God and His church far more than did
Satan when he tempted the Saviour with the
kingdoms of earth. The devil's attempt was no
more false, and far less hypocritical. But let me
forbear, remembering it is also written, "Judge
not, lest ye be judged."*

Assistance of the Almighty

To the synod of the old-school Presby-
terians of Baltimore, who waited on him
in a body, he said:

I saw upon taking my position here, I was going to have an administration, if administration at
all, of extraordinary difficulty. It was without
exception a time of the greatest difficulty this
country ever saw. I was early brought to a lively
reflection that nothing in my power whatever, or
others, to rely upon would succeed without direct
assistance of the Almighty. I have often wished
that I was a more devout man than I am. Nevertheless, amid the greatest difficulties of my administration, when I could not see any other resort,
I would place my whole reliance in God, knowing
all would go well and that he would decide for
the right.[77]

Pisgah and Calvary

Mr. Lincoln was often warned against the danger of assassination. While he never showed any fear, there is no doubt that, from the day of his election to the day of his death, he not only believed that it might be, but actually expected it.

The Rev. Father Charles Chiniquy, who had known Mr. Lincoln in Illinois, visited him at the White House in August, 1861; June, 1862; and June, 1864, for the express purpose of telling him what he had learned of plans to assassinate him. The last visit was on June 9, 1864, when he spent considerable time with him. After Father Chiniquy had explained all, Mr. Lincoln replied in part as follows:

You are not the first to warn me against the dangers of assassination. My ambassadors in Italy, France, and England, as well as Professor Morse, have, many times, warned me against the plots of murderers whom they have detected in those different countries. But I see no other safeguard against these murderers, but to be always ready to die, as Christ advises it. As we must all die sooner or later, it makes very little difference to me whether I die from a dagger plunged through the heart or from an inflammation of the lungs. Let me tell you that I have, lately, read a message in the Old Testament which has made a profound, and, I hope, a salutary impression on me. Here is that passage.

The President took his Bible, opened it at the third chapter of Deuteronomy, and read from the 22d to the 27th verse:

"22 Ye shall not fear them: for the Lord your God he shall fight for you.

"23 And I besought the Lord at that time, saying,

"24 O Lord God, thou hast begun to shew thy servant thy greatness, and thy mighty hand: for what God is there in heaven or in earth, that can do according to thy works, and according to thy might?

"25 I pray thee, let me go over, and see the good land that is beyond Jordan, that goodly mountain, and Lebanon.

"26 But the Lord was wroth with me for your sakes, and would not hear me: and the Lord said unto me, Let it suffice thee; speak no more unto me of this matter.

"27 Get thee up into the top of Pisgah, and lift up thine eyes westward, and northward, and southward, and eastward, and behold it with thine eyes; for thou shalt not go over this Jordan."

After the President had read these words with great solemnity, he added:

My dear Father Chiniquy, let me tell you that I have read these strange and beautiful words several times, these last five or six weeks. The more I read them, the more, it seems to me, that God has written them for me as well as for Moses.

Has He not taken me from my poor log cabin, by the hand, as He did of Moses in the reeds of the Nile, to put me at the head of the greatest and most blessed of modern nations just as He put that prophet at the head of the most blessed nation of ancient times? Has not God granted me a privilege, which was not granted to any living man, when I broke the fetters of 4,000,000 of men, and made them free? Has not our God given me the most glorious victories over my enemies? Are not the armies of the Confederacy so reduced to a handful of men, when compared to what they were two years ago, that the day is fast approaching when they will have to surrender?

Now, I see the end of this terrible conflict, with the same joy of Moses, when at the end of his trying forty years in the wilderness; and I pray my God to grant me to see the days of peace and untold prosperity, which will follow this cruel war, as Moses asked God to see the other side of Jordan,

and enter the Promised Land.   But, do you know,
that I hear in my soul, as the voice of God, giving
me the rebuke which was given to Moses?

Yes! every time that my soul goes to God to
ask the favor of seeing the other side of Jordan,
and eating the fruits of that peace, after which
I am longing with such an unspeakable desire, do
you know that there is a still but solemn voice
which tells me that I will see those things only
from a long distance, and that I will be among the
dead when the nation, which God granted me to
lead through those awful trials, will cross the Jordan,
and dwell in that Land of Promise, where peace,
industry, happiness, and liberty will make every
one happy; and why so?   Because He has already
given me favors which He never gave, I dare say,
to any man in these latter days.

·Why did God Almighty refuse to Moses the
favor of crossing the Jordan, and entering the
Promised Land?   It was on account of the nation's
sins!   That law of Divine retribution and justice,
by which one must suffer for another, is surely a
terrible mystery.   But it is a fact which no man
who has any intelligence and knowledge can deny.
Moses, who knew that law, though he probably
did not understand it better than we do, calmly
says to his people: "God was wroth with me for
your sakes."

But, though we do not understand that mysterious and terrible law, we find it written in letters
of tears and blood wherever we go.   We do not

read a single page of history without finding un-
deniable traces of its existence.

Where is the mother who has not shed real tears
and suffered real tortures, for her children's sake?

Who is the good king, the worthy emperor, the
gifted chieftain, who has not suffered unspeakable
mental agonies, or even death, for his people's
sake?

Is not our Christian religion the highest expression of the wisdom, mercy, and love of God! But
what is Christianity if not the very incarnation of
that eternal law of Divine justice in our humanity?

When I look on Moses, alone, silently dying on
the Mount Pisgah, I see that law, in one of its
most sublime human manifestations, and I am
filled with admiration and awe.

But when I consider that law of justice, and
expiation in the death of the Just, the divine Son
of Mary, on the Mount of Calvary, I remain mute
in my adoration. The spectacle of the Crucified
One which is before my eyes is more than sublime,
it is divine! Moses died for his People's sake,
but Christ died for the whole world's sake! Both
died to fulfill the same eternal law of the Divine
justice, though in a different measure.

Now, would it not be the greatest of honors and
privileges bestowed upon me, if God in His infinite
love, mercy, and wisdom would put me between
His faithful servant, Moses, and His eternal Son,
Jesus, that I might die as they did, for my nation's
sake!

My God alone knows what I have already suffered for my dear country's sake. But my fear is that the justice of God is not yet paid. When I look upon the rivers of tears and blood drawn by the lashes of the merciless masters from the veins of the very heart of those millions of defenseless slaves, these two hundred years; when I remember the agonies, the cries, the unspeakable tortures of those unfortunate people to which I have, to some extent, connived with so many others a part of my life, I fear that we are still far from the complete expiation. For the judgments of God are true and righteous.

It seems to me that the Lord wants to-day, as He wanted in the days of Moses, another victim— a victim which He has himself chosen, anointed and prepared for the sacrifice, by raising it above the rest of His people. I cannot conceal from you that my impression is that I am the victim. So many plots have already been made against my life, that it is a real miracle that they have all failed. But can we expect that God will make a perpetual miracle to save my life? I believe not.

But just as the Lord heard no murmur from the lips of Moses, when He told him that he had to die before crossing the Jordan, for the sins of his people, so I hope and pray that He will hear no murmur from me when I fall for my nation's sake.

The only two favors I ask of the Lord are, first, that I may die for the sacred cause in which I am engaged, and when I am the standard bearer of the rights and privileges of my country.

The second favor I ask from God is that my dear son, Robert, when I am gone, will be one of those who lift up that flag of Liberty which will cover my tomb, and carry it with honor and fidelity to the end of his life, as his father did, surrounded by the millions who will be called with him to fight and die for the defense and honor of our country.

"Never had I heard such sublime words," says Father Chiniquy. "Never had I seen a human face so solemn and so prophet-like as the face of the President when uttering these things. Every sentence had come to me as a hymn from heaven, rever-berated by the echoes of the mountains of Pisgah and Calvary. I was beside myself. Bathed in tears, I tried to say something, but I could not utter a word. I knew the hour to leave had come. I asked from the President permission to fall on my knees and pray with him that his life might be spared; and he knelt with me. But I prayed more with my tears and sobs than with my words. Then I pressed his hand on my lips and bathed it with tears, and with a heart filled with an unspeakable desolation I bade him adieu. It was for the last time! For the hour was fast approaching when he was to fall by the hand of an assassin, for his nation's sake."[78]

Accepted the War

Replying to a toast at a supper given in his honor in Philadelphia, June 18, 1864, Mr. Lincoln said: "We accepted this war for an object, a worthy object, and the war will end when that object is attained. Under God, I hope that it will never end until that time."[*]

Fessenden's Duty

In the summer of 1864 Secretary Chase resigned from the Cabinet, and Mr. Lincoln nominated William P. Fessenden to succeed him. Mr. Fessenden was not disposed to accept. On July 1, in a personal interview, Mr. Lincoln said to Fessenden: "I believe that the suppression of the rebellion has been decreed by a higher power than any represented by us, and that the Almighty is using his own means to that end. You are one of them. It is as much your duty to accept as it is mine to appoint."[79]

National Prayer Meeting

In compliance with a resolution adopted concurrently by the Senate and House of Representatives, requesting the President to appoint a day of prayer, Mr. Lincoln issued the following proclamation, July 7, 1864. After quoting the words of the resolution, he continues:

Now, therefore, I, Abraham Lincoln, President of the United States, cordially concurring with the Congress of the United States in the penitential and pious sentiments expressed in the aforesaid resolutions, and heartily approving of the devotional design and purpose thereof, do hereby appoint the first Thursday of August next to be observed by the people of the United States as a day of national humiliation and prayer.

I do hereby further invite and request the heads of the executive departments of this government, together with all legislators, all judges and magistrates, and all other persons exercising authority in the land, whether civil, military, or naval, and all soldiers, seamen, and marines in the national service, and all the other loyal and law-abiding people of the United States, to assemble in their preferred places of public worship on that day, and there and then to render to the Almighty and merciful Ruler of the Universe such homages and such confessions, and to offer to Him such supplications, as the Congress of the United States have, in their aforesaid resolution, so solemnly, so earnestly, and so reverently recommended.*

Fourth Special Thanksgiving

The national prayer meeting was followed a month later, September 3, 1864, by a proclamation of thanksgiving, as follows:

The signal success that Divine Providence has recently vouchsafed to the operations of the United States fleet and army in the harbor of Mobile, and the reduction of Fort Powell, Fort Gaines, and Fort Morgan, and the glorious achievements of the army under Major-General Sherman, in the State of Georgia, resulting in the capture of the city of Atlanta, call for devout acknowledgement to the Supreme Being in whose hands are the destinies of nations. It is therefore requested that on next Sunday, in all places of worship in the United States, thanksgiving be offered to Him for His mercy in preserving our national existence against the insurgent rebels who have been waging a cruel war against the Government of the United States for its overthrow; and also that prayer be made for Divine protection to our soldiers and their leaders in the field, who have so often and so gallantly periled their lives in battling with the enemy; and for blessings and comforts from the Father of Mercies to the sick, wounded, and prisoners, and to the orphans and widows of those who have fallen in the service of their country, and that He will continue to uphold the Government of the United States against all the efforts of public enemies and secret foes.*

LETTER TO A QUAKERESS

THE QUAKERS, opposed to both war and slavery, were much perplexed by the war, and Mr. Lincoln fully sympathized with them. He wrote the following letter to Mrs. Eliza P. Gurney, an American lady resident in London and wife of a wealthy Quaker banker, Joseph John Gurney, September 4, 1864:

My esteemed Friend: I have not forgotten— probably never shall forget—the very impressive occasion when yourself and friends visited me on a Sabbath forenoon two years ago. Nor has your kind letter, written nearly a year later, ever been forgotten. In all it has been your purpose to strengthen my reliance on God. I am much indebted to the good Christian people of the country for their constant prayers and consolations; and to no one of them more than to yourself. The purposes of the Almighty are perfect, and must prevail, though we erring mortals may fail to accurately perceive them in advance. We hoped for a happy termination of this terrible war long before this; but God knows best and ruled otherwise. We shall yet acknowledge His wisdom, and our own error therein. Meanwhile we must work earnestly in the best light He gives us, trusting that so working still conduces to the great ends He ordains. Surely He intends some great good to follow this mighty convulsion, which no mortal could make, and no mortal could stay. Your people, the Friends, have had, and are having, a very great trial. On principle and faith opposed to both war and oppression, they can only practically oppose oppression by war. In this hard dilemma some have chosen one horn, and some the other. For those appealing to me on conscientious grounds, I have done, and shall do, the best I could and can, in my own conscience, under my oath to the law. That you believe this, I doubt not, and believing it, I shall receive for my country and myself your earnest prayers to our Father in Heaven.*[80]

Lincoln and the Bible

PROFITABLY ENGAGED

Lincoln's old friend, Joshua Speed, tells of a significant incident that occurred in the summer of 1864. Mr. Lincoln and his family were staying at the Soldiers' Home for a little while, and Mr. Speed was invited to spend the night with them. As he entered the room, Lincoln was sitting near a window intently reading his Bible. Mr. Speed remarked, "I am glad to see you so profitably engaged." "Yes," said Lincoln, "I am profitably engaged." "Well," said Speed, "if you have recovered from your skepticism, I am sorry to say that I have not." Lincoln, looking Speed earnestly in the face, and placing his hand on his shoulder, said: "You are wrong, Speed. Take all of this book upon reason that you can, and the balance on faith, and you will live and die a happier man."[81] At this time Mr. Speed was not a member of any church. Later he joined the Methodist Episcopal Church.

USES CRUDEN'S CONCORDANCE

PROFESSOR ALEXANDER WILLIAMSON, who was for a time a tutor in the President's family in Washington, says, "Mr. Lincoln very frequently studied the Bible with the aid of Cruden's Concordance, which lay on his table."[82]

His private secretary, John G. Nicolay, says: "He praised the simplicity of the Gospels. He often declared that the Sermon on the Mount contained the essence of all law and justice, and that the Lord's Prayer was the sublimest composition in human language."[83]

"He could repeat from memory whole chapters of Isaiah, the New Testament, and the Psalms."[84]

"He could repeat hymns by the hundreds, and quoted Dr. Watts' and John Wesley's verses as frequently as he did Shakespeare."[85]

THE ALMIGHTY DIRECTS IN HUMAN AFFAIRS

MR. L. E. CHITTENDEN, who was register of the treasury under President Lincoln, gives in his Recollections a most remarkable testimony. Says he: "Lincoln's calm serenity at times when others were so anxious, his confidence that his own judgment was directed by the Almighty, so impressed me that I ventured to ask him directly how far he believed the Almighty actually directed our national affairs. After a considerable pause, Lincoln spoke as follows:

" 'That the Almighty does make use of human agencies, and directly intervenes in human affairs, is one of the plainest statements in the Bible. I have had so many evidences of His direction, so many instances when I have been controlled by some other power than my own will, that I cannot doubt that this power comes from above. I frequently see my way clear to a decision when I am conscious that I have no sufficient facts upon which to found it. But I cannot recall one instance in which I have followed my own judgment, founded upon such a decision, where the results were unsatisfactory; whereas, in almost every instance where I have yielded to the views of others, I have had occasion to regret it. I am satisfied that, when the Almighty wants me to do, or not to do, a particular thing, he finds a way of letting me know it. I am confident that it is his design to restore the Union. He will do it in his own good time. We should obey and not oppose his will.'"

"You speak with such confidence," said Mr. Chittenden, "that I would like to know how your knowledge that God acts directly upon human affairs compares in certainty with your knowledge of a fact apparent to the senses—for example, the fact that we are at this moment here in this room."

"One is as certain as the other," answered Lincoln, "although the conclusions are reached by different processes. I know by my senses that the movements of the world are those of an infinitely powerful machine, which runs for ages without variation. A man who can put two ideas together knows that such a machine requires an infinitely powerful maker and governor; man's nature is such that he cannot take in the machine and keep out the maker. This maker is God—infinite in wisdom as well as power. Would we be any more certain if we saw Him?"

"I am not controverting your position," said Chittenden. "Your confidence interests me beyond expression. I wish I knew how to acquire it. Even now, must it not all depend on our faith in the Bible?"

"No," said Lincoln. "There is the element of personal experience. If it did, the character of the Bible is easily established, at least to my satisfaction. We have to believe many things that we do not comprehend. The Bible is the only one that claims to be God's Book—to comprise his law—his history. It contains an immense amount of evidence of its own authenticity. It describes a Governor omnipotent enough to operate this great machine, and declares that He made it. It states other facts which we do not fully comprehend, but which we cannot account for. What shall we do with them?

"Now, let us treat the Bible fairly," continued Lincoln. "If we had a witness on the stand whose general story we knew was true, we would believe him when he asserted facts of which we had no other evidence. We ought to treat the Bible with equal fairness. I decided a long time ago that it was less difficult to believe that the Bible was what it claimed to be than to disbelieve it. It is a good book for us to obey—it contains the Ten Commandments, the Golden Rule, and many other rules which ought to be followed. No man was ever the worse for living according to the directions of the Bible."

"If your views are correct," said Chittenden, "the Almighty is on our side, and we ought to win without so many losses. . . ."

Mr. Lincoln promptly interrupted him and said: "We have no right to criticize or complain. He *is* on our side, and so is the Bible, and so are the churches and Christian societies and organizations—all of them, so far as I know, almost without an exception. It makes me stronger and more confident to know that all the Christians in the loyal States are praying for our success, and that all their influences are working to the same end. Thousands of them are fighting for us, and no one will say that an officer or a private is less brave because he is a praying soldier. At first, when we had such long spells of bad luck, I used to lose heart sometimes. Now, I seem to know that Providence has protected and will protect us against any fatal defeat. All we have to do is to trust the Almighty, and keep on obeying His orders and executing His will."[86]

After such testimony, if we allow that Lincoln was honest and sincere, who can doubt his faith or proclaim that he was an atheist or infidel? Three things are herein most clearly established: his belief in the Bible as the inspired Word of God, his belief in the fundamental principles and doctrines of the Christian faith, and his faithful endeavor to live according thereto.

COMFORT FROM JOB

A woman at the White House relates an interesting incident of Mr. Lincoln reading the Bible when everything seemed dark:

"One day he came into the room where I was fitting a dress for Mrs. Lincoln. His step was slow and heavy, and his face sad. Like a tired child he threw himself upon the sofa, and shaded his eyes with his hands. He was a complete picture of dejection. Mrs. Lincoln, observing his troubled look, asked:

" 'Where have you been?'

" 'To the War Department,' was the brief, almost sullen answer.

" 'Any news?'

" 'Yes, plenty of news, but no good news. It is dark, dark everywhere.'

"He reached forth one of his long arms and took a small Bible from a stand near the head of the sofa, opened the pages of the Holy Book, and soon was absorbed in reading them. A quarter of an hour passed, and on glancing at the sofa the face of the President seemed more cheerful. The dejected look was gone, and the countenance was lighted up with new resolution and hope. The change was so marked that I could not but wonder at it, and wonder led to the desire to know what book of the Bible afforded so much comfort to the reader. Making the search for a missing article an excuse, I walked gently around the sofa, and, looking into the open book, I discovered that Mr. Lincoln was reading that divine comforter, Job. He read with Christian eagerness, and the courage and the hope that he derived from the inspired pages made him a new man."[87]

READING THE TESTAMENT

"A Mr. Jay states that, being on the steamer which conveyed the governmental party from Fortress Monroe to Norfolk, after the destruction of the Merrimac, while all on board were excited by the novelty of the excursion and by the incidents that it recalled, he missed the President from the company, and, on looking about, found him in a quiet nook, reading a well-worn Testament. Such an incidental revelation of his religious habits is worth more than pages of formal testimony."[88]

READS BIBLE EVERY MORNING

Captain Mix, the commander at one time of Lincoln's bodyguard, was frequently invited to breakfast with the family at the "Home" residence. "Many times," said he, "have I listened to our most eloquent preachers, but *never* with the same feeling of awe and reverence as when our Christian President, his arm around his son, with his deep earnest tone, each morning, read a chapter from the Bible."[89]

After 1857 Mr. Lincoln seldom made a

speech which did not contain one or more quotations from the Bible.

READS HIS MOTHER S BIBLE

A lady staying at the White House says: "It was his custom when waiting for lunch to take his mother's old worn-out Bible and lie on the lounge and read, and one day he asked me what book I liked to read best, and I said, 'I am fond of the Psalms.' 'Yes,' said he to me, 'they are the best, for I find in them something for every day in the week.' "[90]

HIS MOTHER'S WISH

" 'I would rather Abe would be able to read the Bible than to own a farm, if he can't have but one,' said his godly mother. That Bible was Abraham Lincoln's guide."[91]

GOD'S BEST GIFT

September 7, 1864, a deputation of colored people from Baltimore presented him with a Bible. Lincoln replied:

In regard to this Great Book, I have but to say, it is the best gift God has given to man. All the good Saviour gave to the world was communicated through this book. But for it we could not know

right from wrong. All things most desirable for
man's welfare, here and hereafter, are to be found
portrayed in it. To you I return my most sincere
thanks for the very elegant copy of the great Book
of God which you present.*

SECOND ANNUAL THANKSGIVING DAY

October 20, 1864, Mr. Lincoln issued a
proclamation for a second annual Thanksgiving on the last Thursday in November.
It was in the same reverential and devout
tone as the first one. Since then our Presidents have followed his example by issuing
an annual proclamation, setting apart the
last Thursday of November as a National
Thanksgiving Day. It is as follows:

It has pleased Almighty God to prolong our
national life another year, defending us with His
guardian care against unfriendly designs from
abroad, and vouchsafing to us in His mercy many
and signal victories over the enemy, who is of
our own household. It has also pleased our Heavenly
Father to favor as well our citizens in their homes
as our soldiers in their camps, and our sailors on
the rivers and seas, with unusual health. He has
largely augmented our free population by emancipation and by immigration, while he has opened to
us new sources of wealth, and has crowned the
labor of our working-men in every department of

industry with abundant rewards. Moreover, He has been pleased to animate and inspire our minds and hearts with fortitude, courage, and resolution sufficient for the great trial of civil war into which we have been brought by our adherence as a nation to the cause of freedom and humanity, and to afford to us reasonable hopes of an ultimate and happy deliverance from all our dangers and afflictions.

Now, therefore, I, Abraham Lincoln, President of the United States, do hereby appoint and set apart the last Thursday of November next as a day which I desire to be observed by all my fellow-citizens, wherever they may then be, as a day of thanksgiving and praise to Almighty God, the beneficent Creator and Ruler of the Universe. And I do further recommend to my fellow-citizens aforesaid, that on that occasion they do reverently humble themselves in the dust, and from thence offer up penitent and fervent prayers and supplications to the great Disposer of events for a return of the inestimable blessings of peace, union, and harmony throughout the land which it has pleased Him to assign as a dwelling-place for ourselves and for our posterity throughout all generations.*

GRATEFUL TO GOD FOR REËLECTION

November 9, 1864, in response to a serenade at the White House by a club of

Pennsylvanians, on the occasion of his re-election, Mr. Lincoln said:

I am thankful to God for this approval of the people; but, while deeply grateful for this mark of their confidence in me, if I know my heart, my gratitude is free from any taint of personal triumph. I do not impugn the motives of any opposed to me. It is no pleasure to me to triumph over anyone, but I give thanks to the Almighty for this evidence of the people's resolution to stand by free government and the rights of humanity.*

November 10, 1864, in response to another serenade at the White House by the various Lincoln and Johnson clubs of the District, Mr. Lincoln said:

So long as I have been here I have not willingly planted a thorn in any man's bosom. While I am deeply sensible to the high compliment of a reëlection, and duly grateful, as I trust, to Almighty God for having directed my countrymen to a right conclusion, as I think, for their good, it adds nothing to my satisfaction that any other man may be disappointed or pained by the result.*

Lincoln the Comforter

On November 21, 1864, Mr. Lincoln wrote the following letter to Mrs. Lydia Bixby, of Boston:

DEAR MADAM: I have been shown in the files of the War Department a statement of the Adjutant-General of Massachusetts that you are the mother of five sons who have died gloriously on the field of battle. I feel how weak and fruitless must be any words of mine which should attempt to beguile you from the grief of a loss so overwhelming. But I cannot refrain from tendering to you the consolation that may be found in the thanks of the Republic they died to save. I pray that our Heavenly Father may assuage the anguish of your bereavement, and leave you only the cherished memory of the loved and lost, and the solemn pride that must be yours to have laid so costly a sacrifice upon the altar of freedom.[*92]

What but a pious, devoted, consecrated heart, bearing such stupendous burdens, could write such a pathetic and perfect letter of condolence? This letter should be placed with that immortal twenty-line address at Gettysburg, "the high-water mark of sententious eloquence." With these, also, place that wonderful second inaugural address, "the most sublime state paper of the nineteenth century." These three are sufficient to have crowned any man with imperishable fame, but with Lincoln they were but the fruits of inward piety, purity, and sincerity.

"Most Presumptuous Blockhead"

Mr. Noah Brooks tells of a conversation with the President just after his second election. In reply to the remark that he might remember that in all these cares he was daily remembered by those who prayed, not to be heard of men, as no man ever before was remembered, he caught at the homely phrase and said, "Yes, I like that phrase, 'not to be heard of men,' and guess it is generally true, as you say; at least, I have been told so, and I have been a good deal helped by just that thought." Then he solemnly and slowly added, "I should be the most presumptuous blockhead upon this footstool if I had for one day thought that I could discharge the duties which have come upon me since I came into this place without the aid and enlightenment of One who is stronger and wiser than all others."[93]

Go Away a Better Man

At another time he said cheerfully, "I am very sure that if I do not go away from here a wiser man, I shall go away a better man, for having learned here what a very poor sort of man I am." Afterward, referring to what he called a change of heart, he said he did not remember any precise time when he passed through any special change of purpose, or of heart; but he would say, that his own election to office, and the crisis immediately following, influentially determined him in what he called a 'process of crystallization' then going on in his mind."[94]

FOURTH ANNUAL MESSAGE TO CONGRESS

It is worthy of special attention that in every annual message to Congress Mr. Lincoln begins by an acknowledgment of gratitude to God and reliance upon Him. In his message, December 6, 1864, he begins, "Again the blessings of health and abundant harvests claim our profoundest gratitude to Almighty God."*

ONLY HIS DUTY

Only a few months before Mr. Lincoln died he was waited upon at the White House by about two hundred members of the Christian Commission and officers of the army, who had been holding their annual meeting, to thank him for what he had done for the soldiers and sailors. Mr. George H. Stuart, of Philadelphia, chairman, made a short complimentary speech. Mr. Lincoln replied: "My friends, I owe no thanks for what you have done. You owe no thanks for what I have done. You have done your duty. I have done mine. Let us keep on doing our duty, and by the help of God we may yet save our country. I should be glad to take each of you by the hand." He passed around shaking hands with all present. Bishop Janes said, "Let us pray." One who was present says: "We all fell on our knees, and such a prayer as followed seldom has been heard on earth. Mr. Lincoln responded heartily all the way through. It was next door to heaven in the White House that day."[95]

God's Plans His Plans

On another occasion, replying to certain ministers of the Christian Commission, Mr. Lincoln said:

If it were not for my firm belief in an overruling Providence, it would be difficult for me, in the midst of such complications of affairs, to keep my reason on its seat. But I am confident that the Almighty has His plans, and will work them out; and, whether we see it or not, they will be the best for us. I have always taken counsel of Him, and referred to Him my plans, and have never adopted a course of proceeding without being assured, as far as I could be, of His approbation. To be sure, He has not conformed to my desires, or else we should have been out of our trouble long ago. On the other hand, His will does not seem to agree with the wish of our enemy over there [pointing across the Potomac]. He stands the Judge between us, and we ought to be willing to accept His decisions. We have reason to anticipate that it will be favorable to us, for our cause is right.[96]

In Answer to Prayer

Dr. John D. Hill, a well-known physician of Buffalo, was a member of the Sanitary Commission. At a meeting of that organization in the White House one night he congratulated Mr. Lincoln on having originated such a gigantic plan for the care of the sick and wounded soldiers. Mr. Lincoln said:

You must carry your thanks to a Higher Being. One stormy night I tossed on my bed, unable to sleep as I thought of the terrible sufferings of our soldiers and sailors. I spent an hour in agonizing prayer to God for some method of relief, and He put the Sanitary Commission in my mind, with all its details, as distinctly as though the instructions had been written out by pen and handed to me. Hereafter, always thank your Heavenly Father, and not me, for this organization, which has eased so much pain and saved so many lives.[97]

LINCOLN AND CHURCH MEMBERSHIP

Lincoln was always a regular attendant at church after his removal to Springfield, Illinois. His old neighbors all testify to that. While he lived at Springfield, Illinois, he attended the First Presbyterian Church. When he became President he and Mrs. Lincoln attended regularly the New York Avenue Presbyterian Church. He was never a member of any church. In a conversation with Dr. Phineas D. Gurley, his pastor in Washington, he said that he could not accept, perhaps, all the doctrines of his Confession of Faith, "but," said he, "if all that I am asked to respond to is what our Lord said were the two great commandments, to love the Lord thy God with all thy heart and mind and soul and strength, and my neighbor as myself, why, I aim to do that."[98]

LAW AND GOSPEL

HONORABLE HENRY C. DEMING, a member of Congress from Connecticut, relates that when asked why, with his marked religious character, he did not unite with some church, Lincoln said:

I have never united myself to any church, because I have found difficulty in giving my assent, without mental reservation, to the long, complicated statements of Christian doctrine which characterize their articles of belief and confessions of faith. When any church will inscribe over its altars, as its sole qualification for membership, the Saviour's condensed statement of the substance of both law and gospel, "Thou shalt love the Lord thy God with all thy heart, and with all thy soul, and with all thy mind, and thy neighbor as thy self," that church will I join with all my heart and all my soul.[99]

INTENDED TO MAKE A PUBLIC PROFESSION

In his later life, however, it seems that Mr. Lincoln realized his mistake and intended to make a public profession. A Rev. Mr. Willits, according to F. B. Carpenter, the artist, tells of a lady connected with the work of the Christian Commission, who had occasion to have several interviews with the President. One day Mr. Lincoln said to her: "Mrs. B——, I have formed a very high opinion of your Christian character, and now, as we are alone,

I have a mind to ask you to give me, in brief, your idea of what constitutes a true religious experience." The lady stated that, in her judgment, it consisted of a conviction of one's own sinfulness and weakness, and personal need of the Saviour for strength and support; a feeling of the need of divine help, and a seeking of the aid of the Holy Spirit for strength and guidance; that these were a satisfactory evidence of having been born again." Mr. Lincoln was silent and thoughtful. After a few moments he said, very earnestly: "If what you have told me is really a correct view of this great subject, I think I can say with sincerity that I hope I am a Christian. I had lived until my boy Willie died without realizing fully these things. That blow overwhelmed me. It showed me my weakness as I had never felt it before, and if I can take what you have stated as a *test*, I think I can safely say that I know something of that *change* of which you speak; and I will further add, that it has been my intention for some time, at a suitable opportunity, to make a public religious profession."[100]

Mr. Henry C. Whitney, an intimate and close friend of Mr. Lincoln, says, "This statement was made to an eminent Christian lady, and may be relied upon as authentic, and it shows conclusively that *Abraham Lincoln was a Christian*."[101]

OPINION OF A BOSOM FRIEND

MR. NOAH BROOKS, newspaper correspondent, bosom friend of Mr. Lincoln from 1862 until his death, and author of his biography, writes December 31, 1872, as follows: "I have had many conversations with Mr. Lincoln, which were more or less of a religious character, and while I never tried to draw anything like a statement of his views from him, yet he freely expressed himself to me as having a hope of blessed immortality through Jesus Christ. . . . Once or twice, speaking to me of the change which had come upon him, he said, while he could not fix any definite time, yet it was after he came here, and I am very positive that in his own mind he identified it about the time of Willie's death. In many conversations with him I absorbed the firm conviction that Mr.

Lincoln was at heart a Christian man, believed in the Saviour, and was seriously considering the step which would personally connect him with the visible church on earth."[102]

OPINION OF HIS PASTOR

The Rev. Phineas D. Gurley, D.D., Mr. Lincoln's pastor while President, writes: "I have had frequent and intimate conversations with him [Lincoln] on the subject of the Bible and the Christian religion, when he could have had no motive to deceive me, and I considered him sound, not only on the truth of the Christian religion, but on all its fundamental doctrines and teachings. And, more than that, in the latter days of his chastened and weary life, after the death of his son Willie, and his visit to the battlefield of Gettysburg, he said, with tears in his eyes, that he had lost confidence in everything but God, and that he now believed his heart was changed and that he loved the Saviour, and, if he was not deceived in himself, it was his intention soon to make a profession of religion."[103]

HUNGER AND THIRST AFTER RIGHTEOUSNESS

Mr. Lincoln once said to a friend: "I have read the beatitudes of Jesus. I have sometimes thought I might claim the benefit of the one that pronounces a blessing upon those who hunger and thirst after righteousness; if that fails me, possibly I may come in among the peacemakers."[104]

LOVES JESUS

Shortly before his death an Illinois clergyman asked Lincoln, "Do you love Jesus?" Mr. Lincoln solemnly replied: "When I left Springfield I asked the people to pray for me. I was not a Christian. When I buried my son, the severest trial of my life, I was not a Christian. But when I went to Gettysburg and saw the graves of thousands of our soldiers, I then and there consecrated myself to Christ. Yes, I *do* love Jesus."[105]

"Reticent as he was, and shy of discoursing much of his own mental exercises, these few utterances now have a value with those who knew him which his dying words scarcely have possessed."

IMMORTAL WORDS

In that remarkable and ever-memorable second inaugural address, delivered at Washington, March 4, 1865, just six weeks before his death, he gave utterance to these sublime and immortal words:

Both read the same Bible, and pray to the same God; and each invokes His aid against the other. It may seem strange that any men should dare to ask a just God's assistance in wringing their bread from the sweat of other men's faces; but let us judge not, that we be not judged. The prayers of both could not be answered—that of neither has been answered fully.

The Almighty has his own purposes. "Woe unto the world because of offenses! for it must needs be that offenses come; but woe to that man by whom the offense cometh." If we shall suppose that American slavery is one of those offenses which, in the providence of God, must needs come, but which, having continued through His appointed time, He now wills to remove, and that He gives to both North and South this terrible war, as the woe to those by whom the offense came, shall we discern therein any departure from those divine attributes which the believers in a living God always ascribe to him? Fondly do we hope—fervently do we pray—that this mighty scourge of war may speedily pass away. Yet, if God wills that it continue until all the wealth piled by the

bondman's two hundred and fifty years of unre-
quited toil shall be sunk, and until every drop
of blood drawn with the lash shall be paid with
another drawn with the sword, as was said three
thousand years ago, so still it must be said, "The
judgments of the Lord are true and righteous
altogether."

With malice toward none; with charity for all;
with firmness in the right, as God gives us to see
the right, let us strive on to finish the work we are
in; to bind up the nation's wounds; to care for
him who shall have borne the battle, and for his
widow, and his orphan—to do all which may
achieve and cherish a just and a lasting peace
among ourselves, and with all nations.*

"These words show the President still
untouched by resentment, still brotherly in
his feelings toward the enemies of the
government, and still profoundly conscious
of the overruling power of Providence in
national affairs." Well has it been said
that it was a paper whose Christian sentiment and whose reverent and pious spirit
has no parallel among the state papers of
the American Presidents. "His mind and
soul has reached the full development in a
religious life so unusually intense and
absorbing that it could not otherwise than
utter itself in the grand sentences of his

last address to the people. The knowledge had come, and the faith had come, and the charity had come, and with all had come the love of God."

LETTER TO THURLOW WEED

In reply to a letter complimenting him on the inaugural address, Mr. Lincoln writes to Thurlow Weed on March 15, 1865, as follows:

Men are not flattered by being shown that there has been a difference of purpose between the Almighty and them. To deny it, however, in this case, is to deny that there is a God governing the world. It is a truth which I thought needed to be told, and, as whatever of humiliation there is in it falls most directly on myself, I thought others might afford for me to tell it.*

QUAKERESS PRAYING WITH HIM

MR. F. B. CARPENTER relates what was said by a gentleman at a dinner party in Washington during Mr. Lincoln's second administration, in part as follows: "I was up at the White House, having called to see the President on business. I was shown into the office of his private secretary, and told that Mr. Lincoln was busy just then, but would be disengaged in a short time. While waiting I heard a very earnest prayer, being uttered in a loud female voice in the adjoining room. I inquired what it meant, and was told that an old Quaker lady, a friend of the President, had called that afternoon, and taken tea with the President at the White House, and that she was then praying with Mr. Lincoln. After the lapse of a few minutes the prayer ceased, and the President, accompanied by a Quakeress not less than eighty years old, entered the room where I was sitting."[106]

A Strange Triumphal Entry

ADMIRAL PORTER tells of Mr. Lincoln's visit to Richmond, Virginia, April 4, 1865, making the trip by boat. There was a small house on the landing, and behind it were some twelve negroes digging with spades. Their leader was an old man. He raised himself to an upright position as we landed and put his hands up to his eyes. Then he dropped his spade and sprang forward. "Bless de Lawd," he said, "dere is de great Messiah! I knowed him as soon as I seed him. He's been in my heart fo' long yeahs, an' he's cum at las' to free his chillun from deir bondage— Glory, Hallelujah!" And he fell on his knees before the President and kissed his feet. The others followed his example, the news spread, and in a few minutes Mr. Lincoln was surrounded by a crowd of colored people, who had treasured up the recollections of him caught from a photograph, and had looked to him for four years as the one who was to lead them out of captivity.

Mr. Lincoln looked down at the poor creatures at his feet; he was much embarrassed at his position.

"Don't kneel to me," he said; "that is not right. You must kneel to God only, and thank Him for the liberty you will hereafter enjoy."

His face lit up with a divine look as he said these words. In his enthusiasm he seemed the personification of manly beauty, and that sad face of his looked down in kindness upon these ignorant blacks. He really seemed of another world. . . . The crowd of colored people was so great that the President could not proceed. At last he said:

"My poor friends, you are free—free as air. You can cast off the name of slave and trample upon it; it will come to you no more. Liberty is your birthright. God gave it to you as He gave it to others, and it is a sin that you have been deprived of it for so many years. But you must try to deserve this priceless boon. Let the world see that you merit it, and are able to maintain it by your good works. Don't let your joy carry you into excesses. Learn the laws and obey them; obey God's commandments and thank Him for giving you liberty, for to Him you owe all things. There, now, let me pass on."[107]

THE PRESIDENT AND CABINET IN PRAYER

"On the day of the receipt of the news of the capitulation of Lee, as we learn from a friend intimate with the late President Lincoln, the Cabinet meeting was held an hour earlier than usual. Neither the President nor any member was able, for a time, to give utterance to his feelings. At the suggestion of Mr. Lincoln all dropped on their knees, and offered, in silence and in tears, their humble and heartfelt acknowledgments to the Almighty for the triumph He had granted to the national cause."[108]

THE RESURRECTION OF HUMAN FREEDOM

COLONEL JAMES M. SCOVEL, who, during the Civil War, was a State senator in New Jersey, tells this incident about Lincoln: "The last time I saw him he had just returned from Richmond. He beamed and radiated with happiness. A few days after April 9, which was the day of the Appomattox apple tree, he caught me by both hands—a way he had when emotionally exercised—and said (and I will recall these words in my dying hour): "Young man, if God gives me four years more to rule this country, I believe it will become what it ought to be, what its Divine Author intended it to be—no longer one vast plantation for breeding human beings for the purposes of lust and bondage, but it will become a new Valley of Jehoshaphat, where all the nations of the earth will assemble together under one flag, worshiping a common God, and they will celebrate the resurrection of human freedom."[109]

"In God We Trust"

Honorable Schuyler Colfax, Speaker of the National House of Representatives, in a memorial address, April 24, 1865, says: "Nor should I forget to mention here that the last act of Congress ever signed by him was one requiring that the motto, in which he sincerely believed, 'In God we trust,' should hereafter be inscribed upon all our national coin."[110]

His Last Speech

Mr. Lincoln delivered his last speech on April 11, 1865, in response to a serenade at the White House. In that, as in all his speeches, he shows a devout reverence and a sublime trust in God. He said:

The evacuation of Petersburg and Richmond, and the surrender of the principal insurgent army, give hope of a righteous and speedy peace, whose joyous expression cannot be restrained. In the midst of this, however, He from whom all blessings flow must not be forgotten. A call for a national thanksgiving is being prepared and will be duly promulgated.*

The Last Intercessory Prayer

Three days before Mr. Lincoln's death a Quaker lady was visiting him. He asked her to pray with him, and she felt his hand tremble upon hers like a leaf. Afterward he said, "I feel helped and strengthened by your prayers."[111]

Resigned

Mr. Lincoln was frequently warned of the danger of assassination. From the day of his election he seems to have expected it. A little while before the end he said, "I do not consider that I have ever accomplished anything without God, and if it be His will that I must die by the hand of an assassin, I must be resigned."[112]

His Last Day

Honorable Isaac N. Arnold says that Mrs. Lincoln told him that on the day before his death President Lincoln said to her:

"Mary, we have had a hard time of it since we came to Washington; but now the war is over, and, with God's blessing, we may hope for four years of peace and happiness, and then we will go back to Illinois and pass the rest of our lives in quiet."[113]

His Last Words

THE REV. N. W. MINER, who was pastor of the First Baptist Church of Springfield, Illinois, and an old friend and neighbor of Mr. Lincoln, writes as follows: "Mrs. Lincoln informed me that the last day he lived was the happiest of his life. The very last moments of his conscious life were spent in conversation with her about his future plans, and what he wanted to do when his term of office expired. He said he wanted to visit the Holy Land and see those places hallowed by the footprints of the Saviour. He was saying there was no city he so much desired to see as *Jerusalem;* and with the words half spoken on his tongue, the bullet of the assassin entered the brain, and the soul of the great and good President was carried by the angels to the New Jerusalem above."[114]

Testimony of Friends

Is the evidence sufficient? Has the testimony already produced left a single doubt in anyone's mind as to Lincoln's religious beliefs and character? While his own testimony is the strongest and best upon which to base a conclusion, yet it cannot be out of place to hear the opinions of personal friends and eminent men who have made a careful study of Lincoln's character.

MR. WILLIAM O. STODDARD

Mr. William O. Stoddard, his private secretary, bears testimony as follows: "It may be noted, without any surprise whatever, that many intelligent persons who had associated with Lincoln in his earlier years were never, to the end, able to see anything but what may be called their first mental photographs of him, badly taken, on defective negatives. These were at best but surface pictures and contained only something of the man as he was seen before, say, the year 1858. One of his oldest, most inti-

mate professional associates and latest
biographers [Herndon], for instance, was
hardly acquainted with him at all [in his
later life], for he did not see him after 1860.
[The last time was February 10, 1861.]
That he was of God's appointment must
be apparent to any man whose creed contains a confession of a living God, mindful
of human affairs."[115]

HONORABLE ISAAC N. ARNOLD

HONORABLE ISAAC N. ARNOLD, an intimate friend, for several years a member of
Congress from Illinois, in his Life of Lincoln, says: "No more reverent Christian
than he ever sat in the executive chair, not
excepting Washington. . . . From the time
he left Springfield to his death he not only
himself continually prayed for divine assistance, but continually asked the prayers
of his friends for himself and his country.
. . . Doubtless, like others, he passed
through periods of doubt and perplexity,
but his faith in a Divine Providence began
at his mother's knee, and ran through all
the changes of his life. . . . When the
unbeliever shall convince the people that

this man, whose life was straightforward, clear, and honest, was a sham and a hypocrite, then, but not before, may he make the world doubt his Christianity."[116]

FATHER CHINIQUY

FATHER CHINIQUY, who knew Mr. Lincoln in Illinois, and visited him several times in the White House, says: "Lincoln had spent a great part of his life at the school of Christ, and had meditated his sublime teachings to an extent unsuspected by the world. I found in him the most perfect type of Christianity I ever met."[117]

BISHOP SIMPSON

BISHOP MATTHEW SIMPSON, of the Methodist Episcopal Church, who was one of Mr. Lincoln's most intimate ministerial friends, says, "He believed in Christ as the Saviour of sinners, and I think he was sincere in trying to bring his life in harmony with the precepts of revealed religion."[118]

MR. JOHN HAY

MR. JOHN HAY, who was one of President Lincoln's private secretaries, and Secretary of State under President Roosevelt, in an address at the 100th anniversary of the New York Avenue Presbyterian Church, Washington, D. C., November 16, 1903, standing beside President Roosevelt in the Lincoln pew, said: "Whatever is remembered or whatever lost, we ought never to forget that Abraham Lincoln, one of the mightiest masters of statecraft that history has known, was also one of the most devoted and faithful servants of Almighty God who have ever sat in the high places of the world. From that dim and chilly dawn when, standing on a railway platform in Springfield, half veiled by falling snowflakes from the crowd of friends and neighbors who had gathered to wish him Godspeed on his momentous journey, he acknowledged his dependence on God and asked for their prayers, to that sorrowful yet triumphant hour when he went to his account, he repeated over and over in every form of speech his faith and trust in that Almighty Power who rules the fate of men and nations."[119]

Approved of God

President McKinley, in a speech before the Marquette Club in Chicago, February

12, 1896, said concerning Lincoln: "The war had brought them [the people] and him [Lincoln] to a nearer realization of our absolute dependence upon a Higher Power, and had quickened his conceptions of duty more acutely than the public could realize. The purposes of God, working through the ages, were, perhaps, more clearly revealed to him than to any other." Again he said: "He was the greatest man of his time, especially approved of God for the work He gave him to do. History abundantly proves his superiority as a leader, and establishes his constant reliance upon a Higher Power for guidance and support."

INSPIRED OF GOD

MR. HENRY WATTERSON, in his oration before the Lincoln Union of Chicago, February 12, 1895, on Abraham Lincoln as a Man Inspired of God, pays an eloquent tribute to Lincoln's Christian faith and his following divine guidance. Says he:

"Born as lowly as the Son of God, in a hovel; reared in penury, squalor, with no gleam of light or fair surroundings; without graces, actual or acquired; without

name or fame or official training; it was
reserved for this strange being, late in life,
to be snatched from obscurity, raised to
supreme command at a supreme moment,
and intrusted with the destiny of a nation.

"The great leaders of his party, the most
experienced and accomplished men of the
day, were made to stand aside; were sent
to the rear, while this fantastic figure was
led by unseen hands to the front and given
the reins of power. . . . That, during four
years, carrying with them such a weight
of responsibility as the world never wit-
nessed before, he filled the vast space
allotted him in the eyes and actions of
mankind, is to say that he was inspired of
God, for nowhere else could he have acquired the wisdom and the virtue.

"Where did Shakespeare get his genius?
Where did Mozart get his music? Whose
hand smote the lyre of the Scottish plough-
man, and stayed the life of the German
priest? God, God, and God alone; and as
surely as these were raised up by God, inspired by God was Abraham Lincoln; and
a thousand years hence, no drama, no
tragedy, no epic poem will be filled with

greater wonder, or be followed by mankind with deeper feeling, than that which tells the story of his life and death. If Lincoln was not inspired of God, then there is no such thing on earth as special providence or the interposition of divine power in the affairs of men."

His Crowning Glory

The Rev. Dr. Bishop, quoted before, who had special opportunity to know Mr. Lincoln's religious belief, exclaims: "Let the nation know—let the peopled world that beheld in him 'the Great Commoner,' the incarnation of the ideal republic, know— let the coming generations, looking back to him as the representative of the divine idea of free government, know that the crowning glory of Abraham Lincoln was the grandeur of his Christian character. His faith in the living God was the supreme element in his giant personality."

A Transfigured Life

Lincoln has spoken for himself with no uncertain sound, and no man dare dispute it. His friends have borne testimony. His admirers have seen and recognized his sublime faith and trust in God. Through all of his life there was a spirit of deep reverence. As the cares and responsibilities of life and of public duty came upon him with ever-increasing weight he grew more and more into the image of the Master. Every word and every act of his later life was cumulative evidence that he was no longer conformed to this world, but that he was being transformed day by day into the sweetness and purity and perfection of the Father. His whole life was a gradual crystallization of a soul into the marvelous beauty, transparency, and glory of Divinity Himself.

Religious Development

It is impossible to analyze the development of his religious life, but there are marked stages which may be designated as follows:

From 1809 to 1818, a period of nine years, represents his *mother's training.* From 1818 to 1831, a period of thirteen years, might be called *drifting.* The next four years, from 1831 to 1835, was the period of *questioning.* Then for thirteen years, from 1835 to 1848, his religious life seem to be characterized by *indifferentism.* The ten years from 1848 to 1858 are characterized by the honest doubter *seeking* the true light.† From 1858 to 1862, a period of four years, there are unmistakable evidences of a great soul coming into *full fellowship* with his Master. The next three years, 1862 to 1865, he was, in the highest meaning of the term, a *true follower* of Jesus Christ. While the last months of his life are distinctly marked by the *deepening of his spiritual life.*

WELL DONE

Lincoln developed perfect trust in God. He was always a believer in the existence of God. He was always reverent toward

the Bible.   When a child, he said his evening prayer at his mother's knee:

> Now I lay me down to sleep,
>   I pray Thee, Lord, my soul to keep.
> If I should die before I wake,
>   I pray Thee, Lord, my soul to take.

When a lad, he received a dying mother's
blessing; when a young man, he vowed to
the "Eternal God" that if the opportunity
came he would give slavery a crushing
blow; when he accepted the nomination for
President, he implored "the assistance of
Divine Providence"; when elected, he saw
in the result "the providence of God";
when he left his home at Springfield to go
to Washington, he declared that "without
the assistance of the Almighty I must fail";
when he delivered his inaugural address, he
expressed a "firm reliance upon Him who
has never yet forsaken this favored land";
when the battle of Gettysburg was raging,
upon his knees he prayed "mightily" for
victory, and told the Lord "that this was
His war, and our cause His cause"; in his
second inaugural he declared his "firmness
in the right as God gives us to see the
right"; in his last public address, three days

before his death, his first words were those
of recognition of Him "from whom all
blessings flow"; the day before he was
shot he said to his wife, "With God's
blessing, we may hope"; in the last conscious moment of his life, he expressed a
desire to visit old Jerusalem and "see the
places hallowed by the footprints of the
Saviour."

He had intended, as he said, to make a
public profession of religion by uniting with
some church; but, alas! the public profession was deferred too long. The assassin's
bullet came all too soon. "After four
tempestuous years, in the hour of victory,
in an instant, in the twinkling of an eye,
as it were, his career crystallized into that
pure white fame which belongs only to the
martyr for justice, law, and liberty," and
he who had "felt the great throb of the
plain people's hearts every hour that he
was in the White House," the best-loved
man that ever trod this continent, was
"translated by a bloody martyrdom to his
crown of glory, his soul soaring upward to
the God from whom it sprang, holding in
his right hand four millions of broken

fetters," clinking music more sweet and thrilling than harps of gold struck with celestial hands, receiving the approbation of the heavenly Father whom he loved, "Well done, thou good and faithful servant. Thou hast been faithful over a few things; I will make thee ruler over many things. Enter thou into the joy of thy Lord."

"The greatest character since Christ"—*John Hay*.

"HE WAS A CHRIST IN MINIATURE"—*Tolstoy*.

SOURCES OF INFORMATION

* Complete Works of Abraham Lincoln: Speeches, Letters, and State Papers.   John G. Nicolay and John Hay, 1905. This is the largest and most complete work published, although there are many authentic letters not found in it.

In the following references, the full name of the book is given only once, as a rule. Afterward the author's name is used.

The year in which the book was published is given.

The numbers correspond to the index numbers through the book.

[1] The True Abraham Lincoln, William E. Curtis, 1903, p. 374.

[2] Life of Lincoln, Wm. H. Herndon and Jesse W. Weik, 1892, Vol. I, p. 21.

[3] Abraham Lincoln, Charles Carleton Coffin, 1893, p. 20.

[4] Life of Abraham Lincoln, John G. Holland, 1866, p. 436.

[5] Coffin, p. 23.

[6] Herndon and Weik, Vol. I, p. 24.

[7] Herndon and Weik, Vol. I, p. 25.

[8] The Pioneer Boy, William M. Thayer, 1866, pp. 137, 139.

[9] Holland, p. 23.

[10] Holland, p. 30.

[11] Abraham Lincoln: A History, John G. Nicolay and John Hay, 1890, Vol. I, p. 35.

[12] Herndon and Weik, Vol. I, p. 19.

[13] Thayer, pp. 124, 125. Also, Abraham Lincoln and the Downfall of American Slavery, Noah Brooks, 1903, p. 24.

[14] Holland, p. 31.

[15] Life of Lincoln, Ida M. Tarbell, 1902, Vol. I, p. 42.

[16] Life of Abraham Lincoln, Henry Ketcham, 1901, p. 22; Herndon and Weik, Vol. I, p. 47.

[17] The Life of Abraham Lincoln, Isaac N. Arnold, 1885, p. 31.

[18] Herndon and Weik, Vol. I, p. 64.

[19] Several versions are given. Some authors leave out the word "God," and others put the phrase, "by the Eternal God," at the close of the sentence.

[20] McNamar was his real name, McNeil an assumed name. Herndon and Weik, Vol. I, p. 123. Samuel Hill, John McNeil [McNamar] and Abraham Lincoln were all three infatuated with Miss Rutledge, who was attending Mentor Graham's school. Herndon and Weik, Vol. I, pp. 122–127.

[21] Lincoln Scrapbook, Library of Congress, Washington, D. C., p. 64. Mr. B. F. Irwin, to whom this letter was written, had been personally acquainted with Mr. Lincoln for twenty years and was often in his office. Mr. W. H. Herndon, who, it seems, first published the story that

Mr. Lincoln wrote an essay on "Infidelity," says, "I assert this on my own knowledge, and on my own veracity."—Lamon's Life of Lincoln, p. 489. Mr. Herndon was only a boy fifteen years old at that time, living nearly twenty miles from New Salem. The reader may judge for himself.

[22] Herndon and Weik, Vol. I, p. 158.

[23] Tarbell, Vol. II, p. 31.

[24] It was Joshua Speed's mother who presented Lincoln with an Oxford Bible. He was a brother of Miss Mary Speed. Speed was Lincoln's roommate at Springfield for four years, and the most intimate friend he ever had.

[25] Tarbell, Vol. II, p. 31.

[26] Lincoln Scrapbook, Library of Congress, p. 64.

[27] The Rev. William Bishop, D.D., Salina, Kansas, Address on Lincoln's Birthday, February 12, 1897, which was published in a local paper.

[28] The Later Life and Religious Sentiments of Abraham Lincoln, Rev. James A. Reed, pastor First Presbyterian Church, Springfield, Illinois, published in Scribner's Monthly, July, 1873, p. 333.

[29] Scribner's Monthly, July, 1873, the Rev. James A. Reed.

[30] Daily Illinois State Register, Springfield, Illinois, December 10, 1898. Copy in possession of Miss Jeanette E. Smith, granddaughter of the Rev. Dr. Smith.

[31] Scribner's Monthly, July, 1873, p. 338.   The Rev.
James Smith, D.D., then pastor of the church,
to W. H. Herndon, January 24, 1867.   Letter
first published in Springfield Journal, March 12,
1867.

[32] Abraham Lincoln and the Downfall of American
Slavery, Noah Brooks, 1894, p. 126.

[33] Lincoln, the Citizen, Henry C. Whitney, 1908,
p. 327, the famous "Lost Speech."

[34] Lincoln Scrapbook, Library of Congress, p. 64.

[35] Six Months at the White House, Frank B. Carpenter, 1866, p. 125.

[36] Holland, p. 237.

[37] Lincoln, the Citizen, Henry C. Whitney, p. 202.
Life of Lincoln, Ida M. Tarbell, Vol. II, p.
200.   On the occasion referred to, Judge Gillespie was spending the night with Mr. Lincoln
at the latter's home in Springfield, Illinois.
This incident was related by Judge Gillespie's
daughter, Mrs. Josephine Gillespie Prickett,
living at Edwardsville, Illinois.

[38] Characteristic Anecdotes of Lincoln, John G.
Nicolay, by his daughter, Helen Nicolay, Century Magazine, September, 1912, p. 700.   The
Rev. Hale was pastor of the Second Presbyterian Church, Springfield, Illinois, for a quarter
of a century.   He offered the prayer at the
burial service of Lincoln, May 4, 1865.

[39] Weekly Illinois State Journal, Springfield, Illinois, February 13, 1861.

There is another version of the address, which was given to the papers at the time by a newspaper correspondent, Henry J. Villard.

The speech was extemporized. Both versions are practically the same in thought, but the version used in this book seems more like Mr. Lincoln's style of language.

[40] Words of Lincoln, O. H. Oldroyd, 1895, p. 56.

[41] Life and Public Services of Abraham Lincoln, Henry J. Raymond, 1865, p. 149.

[42] Raymond, p. 151.

[43] Raymond, p. 152.

[44] Recollections of President Lincoln and His Cabinet, L. E. Chittenden, 1891, p. 76.

[45] Lincoln Scrapbook, Library of Congress, Letter of Rev. N. W. Miner, August 1, 1871, p. 52. Mrs. Lincoln told it to Rev. Miner. Mr. Miner was pastor of the First Baptist Church in Springfield, Illinois. He first became acquainted with Mr. Lincoln in 1855. He lived on the same street, on the opposite corner, and saw him almost daily when at home until he went to Washington.

[46] Herndon and Weik, Vol. II, p. 223. Mrs. Lincoln told W. H. Herndon in interview in Springfield, Illinois, September 4, 1866.

[47] Behind the Scenes, Elizabeth Keckley, 1868, p. 103. She was thirty years a slave and four years in the White House, as modiste and friend to Mrs. Lincoln.

[48] Lincoln Scrapbook, Library of Congress, Letter of Mrs. Rebecca R. Pomeroy, p. 54. Mrs. Pomeroy was about fifty years old, living at Chelsea, Massachusetts. She had just buried her husband, the last of her family. She was cultured and graceful, devoutly religious, a member of the Baptist Church. There was a call for nurses for the soldiers' hospitals in Washington. Mrs. Pomeroy felt that it was an opening of Providence, volunteered for service, and was accepted. After she had been there a few weeks, she was selected to nurse President Lincoln's children. Willie died, but Thomas, known as "Tad," recovered. At Mr. Lincoln's request, Mrs. Pomeroy stayed at the White House several months after the boy's recovery.

[49] Carpenter, pp. 117–119.

[50] Lincoln Scrapbook, Library of Congress, Rev. N. W. Miner, August 1, 1871, p. 52.

[51] North American Review, December, 1896, p. 667, James F. Wilson.

[52] Carpenter, p. 282.

[53] Sermons on the Death of Abraham Lincoln, with Funeral Sermon at the White House by Rev. Dr. Gurley, 1865, p. 23.

[54] Complete Works of Abraham Lincoln, Nicolay and Hay, Vol. X, p. 149, foot-note.

[55] Lincoln Scrapbook, Library of Congress, Mrs. Rebecca R. Pomeroy, p. 54. Referred to on p. 80, as "A Christian Nurse."

[56] The author called upon Mr. Scoville at his law office in Philadelphia on October 29, 1912. He confirmed the accuracy of the story as here given, saying it is what his grandmother told him.

In reply to a letter from the Rev. David G. Downey, D.D., Book Editor of The Methodist Book Concern, New York city, December 13, 1912, Mr. Scoville wrote: "Dr. Johnson showed me his manuscript in regard to the Lincoln episode. I told him that this story had been related to me by my grandmother, Mrs. Henry Ward Beecher, and I had no further knowledge as to its truth than that. It has been strenuously denied and also defended. It has always seemed to me to be a perfectly possible situation. It has never, however, been corroborated by any of the members of the family. It rests entirely upon the statement of Mrs. Beecher in her old age."

[57] Lincoln Scrapbook, Library of Congress, Mrs. Rebecca R. Pomeroy, p. 54. Referred to on p. 80 as "A Christian Nurse."

[58] Carpenter, p. 89; Holland, p. 394. This incident is related both by Secretary Chase and Secretary Welles in their published diaries.

[59] Scribner's Monthly, July, 1873, p. 342, the Rev. J. A. Reed.

[60] Life on the Circuit with Lincoln, Henry C. Whitney, 1892, p. 595.

[61] Abraham Lincoln, the Patriot and Christian, Dr. O. F. Presbrey, January 15, 1900, the only one of the seven living at that time.

[62] The Religion of Abraham Lincoln, Charles H. T. Collis, 1900, p. 23. Mr. Munsell had known Mr. Lincoln since he [Munsell] was fifteen years old. Mr. Lincoln often stopped at his father's home.

[63] Men and Things I Saw in Civil War Days, General James F. Rusling, 1899, p. 15.

[64] Lincoln Scrapbook, Library of Congress, Mrs. Rebecca R. Pomeroy, p. 54. Referred to on p. 80 as "A Christian Nurse."

[65] Holland, p. 435.

[66] Anecdotes and Reminiscences, Frank B. Carpenter (in Life of Lincoln, H. J. Raymond), 1865, p. 732.

[67] Curtis, p. 383.

[68] Homiletic Review, 1909, Vol. LVII, p. 156.

[69] Curtis, p. 385.

[70] New York Daily Tribune, April 30, 1870, Letter of Rev. John Tyler, Newark, New Jersey, April 23, 1870.

[71] Scribner's Monthly, July, 1873, p. 340, the Rev. J. A. Reed.

[72] Fifty Years in the Church of Rome, Father Chiniquy, 1886, p. 693.

[73] Carpenter, p. 209.

[74] Chittenden, p. 445.

[75] Holland, p. 432.

[76] The Independent, 1900, p. 435, Helen Everston Smith, who was one of the company.

[77] The Lincoln Memorial Album of Immortelles, Osborn H. Oldroyd, 1883, p. 254.

[78] Chiniquy, pp. 706–710. Everyone ought to read Chapters LX and LXI, pp. 668–735, in Chiniquy's Fifty Years in the Church of Rome. It is a most remarkable story.

[79] Chittenden, p. 382.

[80] Mrs. Eliza P. Gurney, the same lady mentioned on p. 97, in "Reply to Quakers." Some authors have confused the name Gurney with Gurley (Mr. Lincoln's pastor). This probably accounts for the confusion in dates by several authors. The dates here given are authentic.

[81] Lincoln, the Citizen, Henry C. Whitney, 1908, p. 201.

[82] Lincoln's Use of the Bible, S. Trevena Jackson, 1909, p. 8.

[83] Curtis, p. 387.

[84] Harper's Magazine, 1865, Vol. XXXI, p. 226, Noah Brooks.

[85] Curtis, p. 379.

[86] Chittenden, pp. 448–450.

[87] Keckley, p. 118.

[88] Carpenter (in Raymond), p. 734. This incident is taken out of its chronological order. It occurred in 1862.

[89] Carpenter, p. 261.

[90] Lincoln Scrapbook, Library of Congress, Mrs. Rebecca R. Pomeroy, p. 54. Referred to on p. 80 as "A Christian Nurse."

[91] Life and Times of Abraham Lincoln, L. P. Brockett, 1865, p. 743, Sermon by Rev. Joseph P. Thompson, D.D., Broadway Tabernacle, New York City, April 30, 1865.

[92] There were two Bixby families in Massachusetts represented in the war. Five Bixbys were killed, and it was thought they were the sons of Mrs. Lydia Bixby. Afterward three of her sons returned (she had six in the war).—"A Rare Lincoln Letter and Its Curious Story," Boston Sunday Globe, April 12, 1908.

[93] Harper's Magazine, 1865, Vol. XXXI, p. 226, Noah Brooks.

[94] Harper's Magazine, 1865, Vol. XXXI, p. 226, Noah Brooks.

[95] Holland, p. 439.

[96] Holland, p. 440.

[97] The Globe, New York City, February 13, 1911, Rev. Ferdinand C. Iglehart, D.D. In a letter to the author, he says: "Dr. Hill was a member of my Official Board at Delaware Avenue M. E. Church, in Buffalo, while I was pastor, and one of the leading practitioners of the city. The incident is absolutely authentic, as the story came directly from the lips of the reliable man to whom Lincoln spoke the words of beauty and Christian faith."

[98] Scrapbook.

[99] Eulogy of Abraham Lincoln, Hon. Henry C. Deming, before Legislature of Connecticut, June 8, 1865, p. 42.

[100] Carpenter, p. 187.

[101] Life on the Circuit with Lincoln, Henry C.Whitney, p. 281.

[102] Scribner's Monthly, July, 1873, Letter from Noah Brooks to the Rev. J. A. Reed.

[103] Scribner's Monthly, July, 1873, p. 339.

[104] Notebook.

[105] Lincoln Memorial Album, O. H. Oldroyd, 1883, p. 366.

[106] Carpenter, p. 191.

[107] Incidents and Anecdotes of the War, Admiral Porter, p. 295.

[108] Carpenter (in Raymond), p. 735. Quoted in the works of a score of historians and biographers, and almost universally accepted as an historic fact. However, it is only fair to history to say that no Cabinet meeting was held on the day the news was received of Lee's surrender. Mr. Lincoln returned to Washington from Richmond on Palm Sunday, April 9. The news of Lee's surrender was received later on the same day. There was no Cabinet meeting that night. It seems that Secretary Welles was the only Cabinet officer who saw Mr. Lincoln that evening. The incident related probably occurred at an informal gathering of the Cabinet the following morning.

[109] Scrapbook

[110] Life and Principles of Abraham Lincoln, Hon. Schuyler Colfax, 1865, p. 25.

[111] "Cartland's Southern Heroes," quoted by Henry Bryan Binns in his Abraham Lincoln, p. 321.

[112] Life on the Circuit with Lincoln, Henry C. Whitney, 1892, p. 278.

[113] Life of Abraham Lincoln, Isaac N. Arnold, 1885, p. 429. Mr. Arnold and Mr. Lincoln had been personal friends for a quarter of a century, having practiced law together in Springfield, Illinois.

[114] Lincoln Scrapbook, Library of Congress, Rev. N. W. Miner, p. 52. The Rev. Mr. Miner visited Mr. Lincoln and family at the White House and often visited Mrs. Lincoln after the President's death. He was one of the officiating clergymen at the burial of Mr. Lincoln, reading the Scriptures at the grave, May 4, 1865.

[115] The author called upon Mr. William O. Stoddard at his home in Madison, New Jersey, on February 25, 1913. He indorsed the quotation as given.

[116] Arnold, pp. 446–8.

[117] Chiniquy, p. 711.

[118] Our Martyr President: Voices from the Pulpit of New York and Brooklyn—Funeral Oration by Bishop Simpson, 1865, p. 404.

[119] Centennial Volume, New York Avenue Presbyterian Church, Washington, D. C., 1903, p. 97.

† It is this period to which we must date some of
his deepest convictions. Indeed, his pastor,
Dr. Smith, seems to think that he was gen-
uinely converted.

DOCTRINAL BELIEFS AND RELIGIOUS HABITS

The following references will be found helpful to those who may wish to make a more careful study of Mr. Lincoln's doctrinal beliefs, as revealed in his utterances, and of his religious habits, as shown by authentic incidents.

NAMES OF THE DEITY

In referring to the Deity, Mr. Lincoln used no less than *forty-nine* designations. This is very significant, revealing, as it does, the breadth of his thinking and showing how full was his conception of God and His attributes.

The page on which the name first occurs is given.

Almighty, 40
Almighty Architect, 38
Almighty Arm, 70
Almighty Father, 123
Almighty God, 71
Almighty Hand, 125
Almighty Power, 109
Almighty Ruler of Nations, 74

Christ, 66
Creator, 58
Crucified One, 140

Disposer, 159
Divine Author, 179
Divine Being, 87
Divine Majesty, 124
Divine Providence, 60
Divine Will, 99

Eternal God, 30

INDEX

RECOMMENDED FURTHER READING

If you liked this book, the editors of Mott Media suggest that you order one or more of the following biographies of famous Christians. You can order from your bookstore, or by sending a check with the coupon furnished below.

GEORGE WASHINGTON THE CHRISTIAN

George Washington was God's man of the hour. His military and political success was motivated by his consistent faith that God was controlling the majestic event of which he was a part. This book completes the profile of the man who was "First in the hearts of his countrymen."

Softcover trade... 3.95

ROBERT E. LEE THE CHRISTIAN

Robert E. Lee is revealed as a deeply religious man who sought God's will in the decisions which were forced upon him. Throughout the turmoil of conflict, he remained consistent to his God and Saviour. His true Christian character presents a challenge to every believer today.

Softcover trade... 3.95

FOR YOUNG READERS AGES 8-12

ISAAC NEWTON

John Tiner's biography of Isaac Newton fills a gap in our knowledge and understanding of the spiritual life of a man who is usually recognized only for his scientific achievements. His inventions have overshadowed his lifelong practice of Bible study and prayer.   Hardcover... 5.95

B

J.

3 weeks borrowing time

First Congregational Church
LIBRARY
Stoneham, Mass.